5/99

①

HT 8
JP 2

with

# Coping

# DATE AND ACQUAINTANCE RAPE

Andrea Parrot, Ph.D.

THE ROSEN PUBLISHING GROUP, INC./NEW YORK

Published in 1988, 1993, 1995, 1999 by The Rosen Publishing Group, Inc.
29 East 21st Street, New York, NY 10010

*Cover Photo by John Bentham*

**Revised Edition 1999**

**Library of Congress Cataloging-in-Publication Data**

Parrot, Andrea.
    Coping with date rape & acquaintance rape / Andrea Parrot.—rev. ed.
    Includes bibliography and index.
    ISBN 0-8239-2861-6
    1. Rape—United States—Prevention. 2. Dating (Social customs).
3. Sexual ethics. 4. Youth—United States—Sexual behavior. 5. Rape
victims—Services for—United States. I. Title. II. Title: Coping with date
rape and acquaintance rape. III. Title: Date rape.
    HV6561.P37    1995
    362.8'.0088—dc19                                                88-1873
                                                                    CIP
                                                                    AC

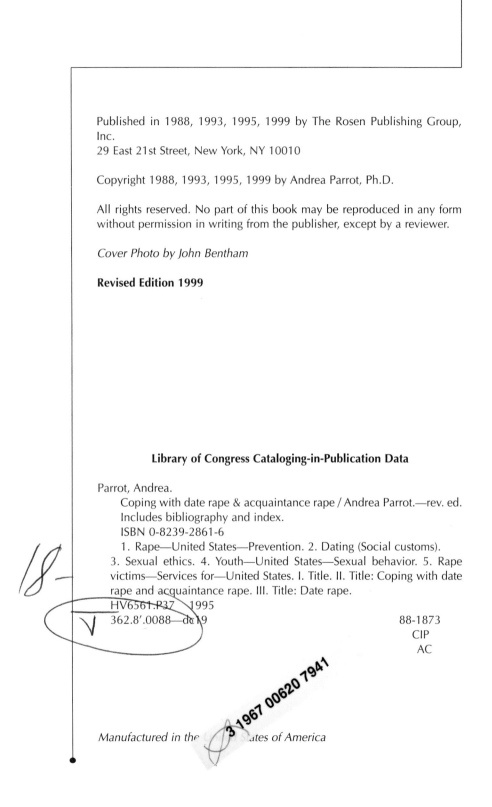

*Manufactured in the United States of America*

## About the Author

Dr. Andrea Parrot, a member of the faculty of Cornell University, focuses her professional work on acquaintance rape prevention and human sexuality. At Cornell she teaches a course on Human Sexuality and Social Policy. She is also a Clinical Assistant Professor of Psychiatry at the SUNY Health Sciences Center of Syracuse, New York, where she teaches a medical school course on Sexuality. She also teaches a women's self-defense course and several graduate courses.

A 1980 Cornell University Edward Sheldon Scholar, Dr. Parrot has been a consultant to numerous colleges, universities, educational media producers, federal and state agencies, and crime prevention programs. She was awarded the 1987 Distinguished Teaching Award at Cornell. Dr. Parrot is a long-standing member of the Education Committee of Planned Parenthood of Tompkins County, New York, and was a founding member of the Cornell University Sexual Assault Prevention Coalition. Her manual *Acquaintance Rape and Sexual Assault Prevention* is viewed as a leading work in the field and has been recommended by *Ms.* magazine. She is also coeditor of *Acquaintance Rape: The Hidden Crime,* and coauthor of *Rape Crisis on Campus: The Problems and the Solutions* and *Rape 101: Sexual Assault Prevention for College Athletes.*

## Acknowledgments

A book on acquaintance rape is difficult to write because many people don't understand the issue and many don't want to. That may be because once we confront the reality of acquaintance rape, we must confront the possibility that we may have been or will be involved in it. Therefore, it is important to present the information in such a way that people can hear it without being frightened or turned off.

Several people were very valuable to me in this effort. All of those who gave me feedback and comments on the manuscript had special expertise as survivors, educators, professionals working with the issue, or as teenagers interested in making the world safer for themselves and others. Among those who provided tremendous insights and understanding were Stephen V. Allen, Jr., M.D., Nina Cummings, M.S., Tim Marchell, M.D.I.V., M.P.H., Marguerite Duane, B.S., Carol Bohmer, J.D., Ph.D., and Rosalind Kenworthy, M.S. In addition, I owe thanks to Stephanie Lampert, Julie Allen, Renee Vargason, Janet Salmons-Rue, John Simon, and Daniel Allen for their patient comments and help in making the book appropriate for young people who have been or are at risk of being raped by acquaintances.

I am especially grateful to all the survivors of date and acquaintance rape who agreed to be interviewed. They have told their stories so that I could share them with you. All the case studies really happened, but some of the details (for example, people's names) have been changed.

# Contents

# Introduction

If you are reading this book, you may have been the victim of sexual harassment, date rape, or acquaintance rape. If so, you have faced some difficult emotions. Few people around you understand what you are going through, or even that you have been assaulted. You may not even be sure exactly what happened to you, or who was to blame.

You are sure that something is wrong. Things are not the same as they used to be. Interpersonal relationships are strained—with peers, because you don't know whom you can trust, and with your family, because you don't know how they will react. You want to be able to tell someone and get help to make things the way they used to be, but you don't know how.

This book will help you with those concerns. You will learn how to cope with the aftermath of date or acquaintance rape, where you can go for help, what you can expect from others, and what you can do to avoid being in a similar situation again.

The book is not for females only. Males also may experience sexual harassment, or date or acquaintance rape, or sexual assault (the term varies from state to state). If you are a male victim, you are not alone. Others have been through it, and others can help you cope with your feelings and needs.

As a male, you may think that your "macho" behavior toward women is acceptable, even if you have pushed some young woman to have sex when she said no. Chapter 15 will help you understand what that type of behavior means to the woman you "pushed." In addition, you will learn new ways of interacting with women so that you don't have to force them to have sex.

Rape is a difficult issue to cope with, but by learning useful skills and increasing your understanding, you cope.

# Date Rape Today

## Tara

Tara, a high school junior, arrived at a party around 10 PM with one of her friends, Sue. The party was at the house of some guys who went to a local college. They were serving beer and chips, and the music was very loud. Tara and Sue didn't recognize many of the people there, until Sue noticed Tim, the guy who had invited her. He was a friend of her older brother. Tim got beers for Tara and Sue and introduced them to a couple of the other guys in the house. He spent a lot of time talking with Tara, while one of his housemates took Sue over to the pool table for a game.

After Tara finished her first beer, Tim offered to get her a refill. She gladly accepted, so she wouldn't feel awkward. Tara wasn't usually a heavy drinker, but she could handle at least three beers without getting really drunk. Tara was planning on sipping the second drink so she wouldn't get buzzed so fast. After a few sips, she began to feel very strange. She told Tim that she needed to sit down. He took her arm and helped her to the sofa in the living room. Tara's vision started to get very fuzzy, she became confused, and then she passed out.

The next thing she knew, Tara was back at Sue's

*house, and it was light outside. She didn't remember anything from last night after she had passed out. She was groggy and was sore between her legs. When Tara realized that her underpants were on inside-out, she panicked. She asked Sue how she had gotten there and what happened at the party.*

*Sue told Tara that she lost track of her at the party and became worried when she couldn't find her. Sue started searching the house and found Tara asleep with her clothes off on a bed in an upstairs bedroom at around 11:30. Sue dressed Tara and tried to wake her up. When she couldn't, she got one of the guys at the party to help carry Tara to the car. Sue took Tara home with her to spend the night, which was their original plan. Sue's brother helped get Tara into the house when they got home. Sue was worried when she couldn't wake Tara, but she didn't want to tell her parents for fear that Tara would get in trouble for being drunk.*

## Rohypnol—The "Date Rape Drug"

What happened at the party? Tara was raped. Rape is defined as (1) forced sexual intercourse, (2) sexual intercourse against the victim's will and without his or her consent, (3) sexual intercourse if the victim is mentally or physically incapacitated, or (4) sexual intercourse if the victim is under the age of consent. Tara had been drugged with Rohypnol, a drug also known as ruffies, roofies, rophies, R2, roofenol, Roche, roachies, la rocha, rope, and rib.

In this case, the victim was mentally incapacitated because she was unconscious. As a result, the sexual intercourse is considered rape. An unconscious victim may not suffer the same aftereffects and trauma as someone who was aware when the rape occurred, but that does not make the event any less criminal. If a rape occurs in which the victim is under the effects of Rohypnol, she has no memo- · ry of the event and criminal prosecution of the assailant is very difficult. If the victim has passed out and the assailant says that he believes she would have wanted to have sex with him, or had sex consensually with him in the past, or even that she said she wanted to have sex with him before he drugged her without her knowledge, is it rape? Yes! Sexual intercourse while someone is drugged is legally rape because the victim is not able to provide informed consent. If a woman consents to sex, she is doing so assuming that she will be a conscious participant, and she always has the right to change her mind. She is unable to change her mind when she is unconscious.

## What Is Rohypnol?

Rohypnol is a drug that some people use to force others into sex without their knowledge or consent. Rohypnol—a type of drug called a benzodiazepine, which is produced by Hoffmann-La Roche in Mexico—is a sedative. It has approximately ten to twenty times the potency of Valium. It is odorless, tasteless, and colorless. A rapist uses it by slipping it into the drink of an unsuspecting person. Rohypnol causes a person who ingests it to pass out and have complete memory loss for about twelve hours. There is no telltale sign that the person was drugged, except that the drug is still measurable in the victim's blood and urine.

The drug cannot be detected by a normal toxicological screen or drug test done at most hospitals. A sophisticated test for Rohypnol is available at most major medical centers, but it must be specially ordered.

The drug remains in the victim's blood for a day or two after it is administered. If the victim goes to a hospital that can't conduct the test for Rohypnol, her blood may be refrigerated and tested for the drug at a later date. If the victim waits for several days to seek medical attention, the drug may have been eliminated from her system. Therefore, if there is even a suspicion of having been drugged, the victim should have blood drawn. She can then have the test for Rohypnol run on the specimen or have the blood refrigerated for testing at a later time. Hoffmann-La Roche has a mechanism for definitive testing for the drug, at no cost, for health care practitioners, rape crisis centers, and law enforcement organizations. Because the drug comes from Mexico, it is most common in the southern states, and especially in Mexico and Florida. However, it has been appearing in other parts of the United States, most often in large cities.

## How to Avoid Rohypnol

Alcohol and drugs have been used for many years to get people to have sex against their will or without their consent. In the past, if an assailant put something in a victim's drink that caused her to pass out, it was called "slipping her a mickey." Rohypnol is different because it is so difficult to detect, and a very small amount will render a person unconscious. Because it is tasteless, odorless, and colorless, it is impossible for a person to know if it is in his or her drink.

What should you do if you are at a party and someone gives you a drink? Unfortunately, we now have to guard our drinks, and get them ourselves. Alcohol intensifies the effects of Rohypnol. However, it can also be slipped into a soda. An assailant can drop the drug into any kind of drink at any party. That means that if a woman accepts a drink from someone, it may have been contaminated. Even if she puts her drink down to dance or go to the bathroom, it may be contaminated in her absence. If you are at a party, bar, or nightclub, here are some dos and don'ts to help you avoid Rohypnol:

- Don't accept drinks from casual acquaintances;

- Don't accept drinks that you don't purchase yourself, even from a "friend";

- Drink only bottled drinks and open them yourself or watch the person who is opening them;

- Don't leave drinks unattended;

- Use the buddy system. Always have a trusted friend with you who can help you to safety should you find yourself passing out from a spiked drink.

## What Is Likely in the Future?

Senator Joseph R. Biden, Jr., chief sponsor of the 1994 Violence Against Women Act, introduced legislation in 1998 to strengthen and expand the original law. This new legislation targets the possession of Rohypnol with maximum federal penalties. Although a small dose of the drug usually causes unconsciousness and amnesia, it can also cause agitation and aggressive behavior. High doses can cause coma, respiratory problems, and death.

# The Gray Zone—Who Is at Fault?
# Adam

*In 1996 Adam Lack, a student at Brown University, went into a friend's room at his fraternity house to borrow a CD. In the room he found a woman lying next to a puddle of vomit. Adam invited her back to his room. She was able to walk to his room on her own. He gave her some water and asked her if she wanted to sleep on his bed. She said yes and lay down.*

*Adam also lay down, completely dressed, with his back to her. She started to kiss him, and he kissed her back. Then she started to touch him sexually, and he responded. She asked him to put on a condom, and they had sexual intercourse. After that, she asked if there was anything else she could do for him, and he said yes. He asked for, and she performed, oral sex. Later they talked and smoked cigarettes until it was light outside.*

*Adam called her a few days later, and she told him she didn't remember anything about the intimate time they had spent together in his room. He told her what had happened. When she heard what had occurred, she reported him to university officials and he was charged with sexual misconduct. He was found guilty, and the initial penalty was suspension for six months. However, the charge was reduced to "flagrant disrespect" and the penalty was reduced to probation.*

## What Makes This Rape?

Was the woman the victim of sexual assault? Was Adam treated unfairly? She initiated sexual intimacy, asked him to put on a condom, and asked if there was anything else he wanted after sexual intercourse. Since she initiated sex, why was he brought up on charges?

The law says that if a person is unable to give informed consent, then he or she is mentally incapacitated. This woman had "blacked out" from drinking too much alcohol. A blackout is amnesia, or memory loss, prompted by alcohol. A person can appear to be aware and functional, but his or her speech and actions will be slurred and awkward.

Brown University officials apparently believed that Adam should have known that the woman had consumed too much alcohol to give informed consent. This was because the woman had vomited as a result of drinking too much alcohol. When a person drinks enough to vomit, his or her mental capabilities are compromised. So although the woman initiated sex, university officials apparently believed that Adam should have realized she was incapacitated when he found her passed out near a puddle of vomit. Thus, they believed that Adam was at fault.

## Was He Unfairly Accused and Punished?

Many men in this circumstance would probably feel that they did nothing wrong because their sexual partner was able to walk and talk. Adam did not even initiate sex. He didn't get her drunk. He did not use force. He was being a "gentleman." How could this be rape? How could they charge him with anything? Many men believe that they are expected to be too careful, and that they can't do anything right.

One of the reasons that Brown University was within its rights to charge and convict Adam of wrongdoing was because they were enforcing their campus code of conduct, not the law. Colleges and high schools can, and often do, have higher expectations of acceptable and moral behavior than does the criminal justice system. A school can impose fairly rigid rules on its students in order to maintain social order on campus. And if students violate these rules, they are removed from campus. Attending a particular school is often a privilege, not a right; and schools can and do suspend and expel students who behave in ways the school finds unacceptable.

The lesson we should all learn from this case is that we need to be absolutely sure of the wishes of our partners, and that our partners understand the nature of the intended activities before we engage in any kind of sexual relationship. This requires clear, honest, open communication before any sexual encounter.

The law and most schools' codes of conduct blame the initiator (who is not always the man) if both people are drunk. In our culture, however, the man is very often the initiator, and men need to be especially careful in cases where both people have been drinking.

If one person is too highly intoxicated to be able to give informed consent, then the sober person is responsible for the sexual actions that take place. Both of the stories presented in this chapter are difficult and disturbing. However, they reinforce the importance of making well-informed decisions about relationships and sex, being sure that drugs and alcohol are not part of the equation.

# A Progression of
# Sexual Violence

Adolescence is a time of sexual exploration, in both behavior and attitudes. These explorations sometimes result in encounters that may be pleasant or confusing, and they sometimes result in physically and emotionally painful experiences in the form of both sexual assault and sexual harassment. Most of this book deals with sexual assault in social settings; however, the issue of sexual assault and sexual harassment in the school setting is an important aspect of the problem and is addressed in this chapter.

Young people spend a third of their waking hours in school or in school-related activities. Furthermore, the sexual assault and sexual harassment they experience is not only at the hands of their peers; sometimes the people who commit these offenses are school staff members. Increasing research is documenting these experiences of young people not only in high school, but sometimes in junior high or even middle or elementary school. Young people and their parents are not only acknowledging that these things happen, but they are making them a legal issue.

In a 1993 study of 1,632 U.S. high school students, published by the American Association of University Women (AAUW), the researchers defined specific behaviors as sexual harassment and determined their frequency by asking students the following questions:

"During your whole school life, how often, if at all, has anyone (this includes students, teachers, other school employees, or anyone else) done the following things to you when you did not want them to?

- Made sexual comments, jokes, gestures, or looks

- Showed, gave, or left you sexual pictures, photographs, illustrations, messages, or notes

- Wrote sexual messages or graffiti about you on bathroom walls, in locker rooms, and so on

- Spread sexual rumors about you

- Said you were gay or lesbian

- Spied on you as you dressed or showered at school

- Flashed or mooned you

- Touched, grabbed, or pinched you in a sexual way

- Pulled at your clothing in a sexual way

- Intentionally brushed against you in a sexual way

- Pulled your clothing off or down

- Blocked your way or cornered you in a sexual way

- Forced you to kiss him or her

- Forced you to do something sexual other than kissing

Of the respondents, 81 percent indicated that they had been sexually harassed in school, not taking into account experiences they had suffered in other settings, such as on a date or at work. The 81 percent included both girls and boys. Eighty-five percent of the girls and 76 percent of the boys in grades eight to eleven said they had been the subject of unwelcome sexual behavior at least once in their school careers. Seven percent of girls and 6 percent of boys reported that it had happened before third grade.

Following are a few actual cases of sexual harassment and sexual assault that have occurred since 1993:

### 1993, California

*Nine high school students, members of a gang called the Spur Posse, were arrested on sexual assault charges stemming from the gang's competition for sexual conquests. At the time, only two young men were formally charged, one of whom pleaded no contest to a single charge of lewd conduct with a ten-year-old child. In light of new evidence, however, charges were filed against one of the students who had previously been released.*

### 1994, Illinois

*A thirteen-year-old girl told police that a seventeen-year-old student forced her into a high school bathroom, removed her clothes, and assaulted her. The victim alleges that she had refused the accused.*

### 1994, Illinois

*A sixteen-year-old high school student was charged with sexually assaulting two female classmates after a small party. One of the young women testified that the accused followed her up to her room and began fondling her after she refused to have sex with him.*

## 1995, California

*A seventeen-year-old basketball star was charged with rape and child molestation after allegedly assaulting a twelve-year-old girl.*

## 1995, Ohio

*A ninth-grade high school student alleged that two male peers (ages fifteen and eighteen) took her into the basement of the school and took turns raping her in the coach's office.*

# Sexual Harassment

Sexual harassment is very confusing to many people, even people who should know what behaviors comprise the offense. In the mid-1990s, a six-year-old boy was charged with sexual harassment for kissing a little girl on the playground of their school. He was barred from attending the school's ice cream social as a punishment, even though the girl reportedly said that she wanted him to kiss her. In order for behavior to be considered sexual harassment, it must be unwanted, repeated, and must have the effect of creating a hostile and offensive work or educational environment.

## Long-Term Effects

Sexual harassment, like sexual assault, carries with it many profound and long-term effects. These are both physical and emotional and frequently affect school performance. In her book *Sexual Harassment and Teens,* Susan Smith describes the long-term consequences of sexual harassment. Victims often experience physical effects including: acne, changes in body weight, colds and other illnesses, dependence on alcohol or other drugs, headaches, stomachaches, backaches, other physical aches and pains, eating disorders, nausea, sleeplessness and sleep disturbances, sore throats, and ulcers. Many of these symptoms are the same as those experienced by sexual assault victims.

The mental and emotional problems are also severe, including: anger, anxiety, confusion, depression, detachment, embarrassment, fear, feeling degraded, feeling intimidated, feeling powerless, feelings of dread, guilt, and helplessness, humiliation, irritability, isolation/withdrawal, loss of trust in others, low self-esteem, mood swings, self-doubt, shame, and stress.

These physical and mental problems often lead to difficulty with school performance: excessive absenteeism, "acting out," a damaged reputation, delayed graduation or failure to graduate, drop in quality of schoolwork, dropping of a class, inability to concentrate, distraction, loss of friends, loss of trust in the educational system, tardiness, and truancy.

Many teenage victims of sexual harassment or assault experience the long-term effects far into adulthood. They are likely to experience continued inability to trust others, stress-related physical problems and symptoms, and difficulty acquiring good jobs or college recommendations.

When young people are sexually harassed in school, they should tell someone who is in a position of authority, such as a teacher, coach, guidance counselor, or administrator. If the first person is not able to help, the young person should persist until she or he receives the needed help.

Sexual harassment is a serious and potentially long-term problem. It is common to teenagers both as victims and assailants. Both males and females seem to be at significant risk of being sexually harassed by either peers or adults while in high school or earlier. We must all learn about the behaviors that constitute sexual harassment, because some of those same behaviors contribute to instances of sexual assault.

## The Progression of Sexual Violence

Whenever sex is against a woman's will and without her consent, it is rape. But frequently the assailants' perceptions do not allow them to see it that way. Assailants may view what they did as within the acceptable range of social behavior.

One of the reasons for this view may be failure to understand how other sexist, objectifying, or exploitative behaviors contribute to sexual victimization. The Sexual Violence Progression chart on the next page depicts the relationship between these behaviors.

**Sexist jokes:** Becoming desensitized by hearing sexist jokes makes it easier later to tell similar jokes, especially if the person who told the jokes is held in high esteem. The more the teller of the jokes is respected, the less offensive the jokes are likely to seem.

Peer pressure seems to increase the likelihood for men

17

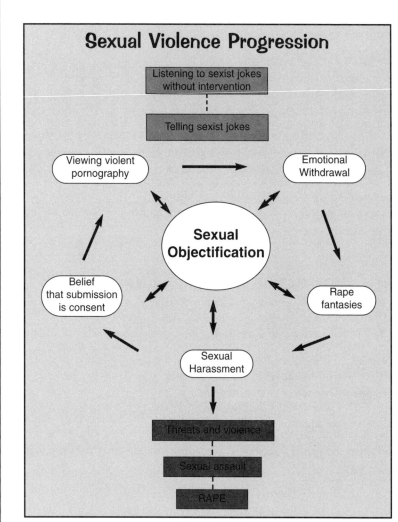

Sexual Violence Progression (In *Rape Awareness and Prevention Model for Athletes*, A. Parrot, N. Cummings, T. Marchell, and J. Hofher, with graphics by Deborah Moore).

to view inappropriate behaviors as acceptable. In the movie *The Accused*, when Jodie Foster is being gang-raped on screen, some audiences are reported to have cheered the rapists on. For some members of the audience, hearing people cheering may reinforce the belief that gang rape is acceptable behavior.

**Sexual objectification:** An example of this behavior is "scoring" women as they walk by. For example, a person may comment that a woman is "beautiful, a 10," or "a real dog, a 2." A woman may be likened to an animal, such as "chick," or barked at because she is such a "dog." This is a form of harassment if the woman hears the comments. Sexual objectification is reinforced by the behaviors that follow, and it also reinforces those behaviors.

**Emotional withdrawal:** A man who withdraws emotionally is likely to be uninterested in his partner's emotional needs and wishes. He may say, "I don't care what you want. What I want is more important."

**Viewing of violent pornography:** Evidence suggests that this desensitizes people to rape and is a central element in the socialization of many rapists. A milder form of violence against women may be seen in music videos and R-rated movies that cater to young audiences. In one such film a woman is gang-raped for half an hour, and in another a naked woman is nailed to a wall with a nail gun. Films of this sort reinforce violence against women.

**Belief that submission is consent:** If a woman stops fighting or saying no, or says nothing, a man may continue to have sex with an unwilling partner.

**Rape fantasies:** Men who have fantasies about rape derive sexual pleasure from violently controlling their partner and may believe that all women secretly want to be raped.

**Sexual assault:** Any forced sexual behavior short of forced sexual intercourse.

**Rape:** Sexual intercourse against the will and without the consent of a victim.

## Conclusion

It is important to understand the relationships between these behaviors, because they will not stop unless people are able to identify them and consciously work toward eliminating them from their lives. We all suffer because of sexual exploitation, sexual harassment, sexual assault, and rape. Women suffer because they are potential victims, and their fear about victimization takes an emotional toll. Those who become victims suffer immeasurably. In addition, the rape of any woman adds to all women's distrust of all men.

All men suffer because men are also potential victims. But it is more likely that a man will be the father, brother, or lover of a victim. Victimization of one's significant other seriously interferes with a normal relationship. Men suffer because rape takes an emotional toll on all who are touched by it. In addition, it is difficult for men to endure the distrust women have for them. Men also have to live with women they love who are forced to limit their options and experiences because of their fear of rape.

Attempted rape carries with it many of the same emotional and physical burdens as completed rape.

Additionally we all suffer economically because of the cost in tax dollars for the court system to handle these cases. The financial cost of psychological treatment of victims is enormous. The incarceration of convicted rapists also incurs a tremendous tax burden. And a more subtle economic cost is the lost wages and time of victims who can't go to work or are unable to do their jobs.

We can and must do something to stop sexual victimization. It is important to our welfare, but also to the welfare of future generations.

# "It Wasn't Rape. He Just Took Advantage of Me."

## Melanie

*During her fourth week at college, Melanie was asked out by a junior who was on the football team. She and all her friends knew that Kurt was one of the most popular and attractive men on campus. Melanie couldn't believe that Kurt would look at her, much less ask her for a date, although they were lab partners in biology class and seemed to get along well when they were working together.*

*Kurt asked Melanie to a party after the first home football game. The party was wild, with lots of beer, loud music, roughhousing, and dancing. It was held at a fraternity house where many of the football players lived. Melanie and Kurt danced together between beers, and Melanie's seductive dancing drew the attention of most of the men there. She didn't notice this because she was rapidly becoming drunk.*

*At one point there was a beer fight, during which almost everyone got wet to some degree, but Kurt and Melanie were drenched. Melanie was very uncomfortable in her wet and smelly clothes. She told Kurt that she had to go home and change. Besides, she was feeling a little uncomfortable about Kurt's kissing and fondling her in front of his friends. She excused* his behavior on the ground that he was so drunk he didn't know what he was doing. She liked kissing him, but not in front of his friends.

Kurt begged her to stay and said she could put on some of his clothes. He had a clean football jersey that was so large it would fit Melanie like a dress. He told her that there was a bathroom upstairs where she could clean up, and she could lock the door. It sounded like a good plan, and she really didn't want to leave. She was having a good time, and she was worried that Kurt would take up with one of the other girls at the party, which might blow her chances to date him again.

After she had changed she met Kurt in his room, where she was going to leave her clothes. Sitting on the bed, he told her that she looked really sexy in that jersey and that she had nice legs. He walked over to her, kissed her, and closed the door. Then he picked her up and carried her over to the bed. She protested that she thought they should go back downstairs and get more beer, but Kurt produced a full pitcher and poured her a glass. Melanie was feeling uneasy, but she did not know how to get Kurt downstairs without sounding like a prude.

Kurt said that he had admired Melanie ever since he had first seen her and was very happy when they were assigned as biology lab partners. He told her that he really wanted to get to know her better. She said that she felt the same way about him and that they should spend more time together. She asked him who his favorite rock star was. He said Madonna because she was sexy and reminded him of Melanie.

*Then he said, "Let's see how well you move to this song," and he put on "Like a Virgin."*

*Kurt pulled the jersey up and tried to fondle and kiss Melanie's breasts. She was feeling really good, but she didn't think that they should be doing anything more than that on the first date. She was afraid Kurt wouldn't want to stop if they went any further. She decided that they could touch above the waist but nothing more, so they continued that for a while. When Kurt started to remove her underpants, she protested vigorously and said that she didn't want to at that time. Kurt got angry and called her a tease. He said he knew she "wanted it" by the way she had danced and responded to his advances. She had danced like Madonna downstairs and had been giving him sexual come-ons all night. She was not going to stop him now.*

*Kurt, who weighed 230 pounds, got on top of Melanie (who weighed 110) and forced her to have sexual intercourse until he came (ejaculated). Then he passed out on top of her. She could not move until he rolled over about half an hour later. She got up, put on her wet clothes, and went home.*

Would you consider this rape? Many people would not, perhaps not even Melanie. She may tell her friends that Kurt took advantage of her, or she may not tell anyone at all. Melanie was a virgin before Kurt forced her to have sex, and she feels terrible about the whole event.

Melanie is likely to blame herself for what happened. She doesn't know how to feel or what to think. She is very confused because she thinks she may have been responsible. After all, she did go to his room voluntarily, did dance very suggestively, was drunk, and she did let Kurt partially undress her and fool around with her. Maybe she was leading him on or teasing him. She shouldn't have gone back to his room, shouldn't have gotten drunk, and shouldn't have let him undress her, but she did. She didn't yell and scream, didn't fight, was not bruised or beaten. Because of all that, very few people would consider this rape. But it was rape!

Melanie was the victim of a typical acquaintance rape. Unfortunately, many people experience acquaintance rape. It is far more common than stranger rape, yet we don't hear about it nearly as often. That is because most people believe that in rape the attacker is a total stranger who jumps out of the bushes and the victim is young, attractive, and financially well off, fights back, is beaten, is hysterical, reports the crime to the police immediately, and has medical evidence collected. Some of those factors are present in stranger rape situations, but fewer of them are present in acquaintance rape. So, because victims of acquaintance rape do not have the commonly accepted rape experience, most people are more likely to believe the victim of stranger rape than of acquaintance rape.

## Myths About Acquaintance or Date Rape

*Myth:* A rapist is always a stranger.

*Fact:* Most incidents of rape happen between two people who know each other. For example, they may be casual acquaintances, dates, friends, family friends, classmates, or fellow workers. Most acquaintance rape happens in one of the two people's home. The Federal Bureau of

Investigation (FBI) has estimated that fewer than one in ten rapes is reported to the police, but most of the reported rapes are stranger rapes. Several studies conducted at colleges and universities indicate that fewer than one in 100 acquaintance rapes is reported to the police.

*Myth:* Women are always the victims.

*Fact:* Both men and women can be victims of rape. Some state laws define rape as something that only a man can do to a woman, but in other states both women and men can be legally considered victims or assailants. Men are victims in approximately 10 percent of all sexual assaults, but men are less likely than women to report being raped. Many men are embarrassed and think others will make fun of them or not believe them. They think men are supposed to be always ready and willing for sex with women. Men are also victimized by other men. They may not report such an assault because they are embarrassed or fear others will think they are homosexual. In fact, rape is violence expressed in a sexual way, and to the victim it is very different from consensual sex.

Because victims are usually women and assailants are most often men, that terminology is used throughout this book. However, the reverse could be true in any situation discussed. Similarly, the situations could occur in homosexual relationships as well as heterosexual ones. Often, the interaction between male and female sex roles contributes to acquaintance rape. Thus acquaintance rape is primarily a heterosexual rather than homosexual phenomenon.

Myth: A woman is truly a rape victim if she is hysterical and bruised.

Fact: Immediately after a rape the victim may be in shock or may be hysterical. Shock is the more common response. The victim is likely to appear calm and collected but is actually suffering from rape trauma syndrome. This is an emotional disorder that requires prompt medical attention. It is discussed in detail in chapter 9.

Most victims of date or acquaintance rape are not bruised, cut, or beaten. The victim often thinks the assailant will come to his senses at any moment. After all, he is a nice guy and wouldn't force her to do anything. She may know him well enough to be aware that he becomes violent when drunk or angry, and therefore she may be afraid to resist or fight back. She may not want to embarrass him or herself by screaming because she is sure he will stop when he realizes what he is doing. She can't believe that anyone who likes her would rape her, and since she thinks he likes her, she thinks he will stop.

Myth: Rape victims are young, attractive, financially well off, and white.

Fact: Any woman can be a victim of rape, and any man can be a victim of sexual assault. Rape happens to women of all social classes, of all ages and occupations. Even prostitutes can be raped, although some believe that if a woman has had sex with hundreds of men she has given up her right to say no.

Many people believe that nobody would willingly have sex with an unattractive woman or an older woman, and that such women would be willing to have sex with anyone.

Similarly, minority and poor women are often rape victims, but they are believed less often than white women or well-to-do women. This train of thought implies that rapists select only women who are sexually attractive, that unattractive women must have "wanted it" and purposely allowed it to happen. That is not true.

Most people don't believe that a man can be the victim of acquaintance rape or sexual assault by a woman because men are supposed to be always ready and willing to have heterosexual sex. If a man is forced by another man, many believe that he should be strong enough to fight off his attacker. In reality, men are forced to have sex by both men and women, but very few ever report the rape in either case.

## Types of Rape

Most date rapes occur because a man has planned to have sex. In other words, the man probably did not plan at the start of the evening to rape the woman, but he did intend to have sexual intercourse with her. Sex would be the perfect end to the evening for him. He may know that his buddies will want a report from him about his sexual experiences the previous night, and he wants to have something to tell them. In addition, he may have been fantasizing about a sexual end to the evening ever since he made the date.

### LaTisha

*Shawn believed that LaTisha had sex with everyone she dated (although the reputation was unfounded), and so he "knew" that she would have sex with him. Since LaTisha asked Shawn out, he thought that*

28

*meant she was "easy" and really wanted to have sex with him.*

*When LaTisha said no to sexual intercourse at the end of the date, Shawn felt teased, tricked, and disappointed. He felt that he had a right to sex, especially because he had spent a lot of money for dinner.*

Shawn interpreted LaTisha's nonverbal signals as indicating that she wanted to have sex too. She had gone to his apartment, they had kissed and "fooled around" (touched breasts and genitals), and they were both sexually aroused.

Not all men would rape given these circumstances. Many men stop if the woman says no but are frustrated and angry because they didn't get what they wanted. The fact that a man is frustrated and angry does not necessarily mean that he will rape.

## Planned Sex That Becomes Rape

In date rape, the man has been planning sex, premeditating sex. If the woman turns him down, he may become angry and do what it takes to get what he wants and thinks he deserves. A man is much more likely to push his date to have sex if he has been drinking (or doing drugs). All other factors being equal, the degree of the man's intoxication is the best predictor as to whether acquaintance rape will occur.

Definitions of rape vary by state. In some states, rape is defined as penile/vaginal contact; in others, all forms of forced sex are considered rape (such as forced oral sex, forced anal sex, and forcing of objects into sexual orifices). Marital status is also a determining factor in rape law in

29

some states. In about half of the states, a woman may not charge her husband or live-in boyfriend with rape. The definitions that follow are general regarding the above factors but outline the differences among acquaintance rape, date rape, marital rape, soft rape, and gang rape.

The meaning of the term "force" may include physical force, threat of force, violence, threat of violence, coercion, or threat of coercion. In most states, if a victim fears for her life or her safety and has sexual intercourse (penetration of penis into vagina) under those circumstances, it is legally considered rape. For example, if a victim has sex because an assailant implies that he has a weapon and is willing to use it, the situation is legally defined as rape even if the assailant does not have a weapon.

Acquaintance rape is forced sexual intercourse (or other sexual act) that occurs between two people who know each other. The relationship can be any acquaintance, including a date, teacher/student, friend of the family, friend, employer/employee, husband/wife, doctor/patient. Date rape is only one form of acquaintance rape.

Date rape is forced sexual intercourse (or other sexual act) that occurs between a dating couple or while on a date.

Marital rape is forced sexual intercourse (or other sexual act) that occurs between husband and wife. Some states do not legally recognize this as rape. Even in states where marital rape is against the law, it is almost impossible to obtain a conviction unless the couple is separated or divorced, or unless some other form of violence such as assault and battery accompanies the rape.

Soft rape is forced sexual intercourse (or other sexual act) in which coercion (mental pressure or intimidation) or threat of coercion is used to gain the victim's compliance.

Gang rape is forced sexual intercourse by more than one assailant. The victim may be unconscious from drinking and may not know she is being raped. She may have consented to have sex with one man and be forced by more.

## Sonia

*Sonia and Darnell were driving in his car at 1 AM in an isolated area about ten miles from the nearest town. Darnell told Sonia that he wanted to show her his favorite spot to "commune with nature." It was winter, very cold, and snowing. Darnell said he liked this spot best with a new snowfall, because it was so pure and clean.*

*Sonia had completely lost her bearings on the way to where they now were. When Darnell stopped the car and started to make sexual advances, Sonia tried to stop him. Darnell said, "The last girl I was with didn't want to have sex with me, so I let her out right here." Sonia knew she would never find her way back before she froze. She also thought that the proverbial stranger rapist might be lurking behind a tree out there in the dark. She had sex with Darnell without further protest.*

This was soft rape because Sonia was fearful for her life and her safety. Darnell did not coerce her, but he threatened coercion. Even if most people would have been able to find their way out of the woods and back to safety, if Sonia could not or believed she could not, the situation was rape. Sonia was coerced because of her fear and lack of survival skills. The way others would have reacted has

31

no bearing on Sonia's situation, because no one else was there to help Sonia. However, others who listen to Sonia's story (such as family, friends, police, district attorney) may tell her it was not rape and blame her, saying that she should have been able to find her way out of the woods or that she shouldn't have let him take her there. Regardless of the opinion of others, Sonia did not feel capable of finding her way out of the woods in safety.

## Stranger Rape

In contrast to acquaintance rape, which is usually a planned attempt to have consensual sex, stranger rape is premeditated rape. Stranger rape usually begins in the mind of the rapist as an attempt to degrade and overpower the victim. Some stranger rape occurs incidentally in connection with another crime, for example, when someone breaks into a house to burglarize but decides to rape the woman who is home. In acquaintance rape, it is sex that is planned, rather than a crime. In acquaintance rape, if sex does not happen as the aggressor planned, rape occurs. The assailant overpowers the victim to get what he wants— sex. He may want to degrade the victim as well.

## Types of Rapists

Nicholas Groth, author of *Men Who Rape*, describes three types of rapists: the power rapist, the anger rapist, and the sadistic rapist.

### Power Rapist

The power rapist rapes to feel powerful. He exerts as much power as needed to rape his victim. If the victim does not resist, very little power is used. If the victim does resist, the rapist exerts as much power as necessary to be successful, so the victim may be bruised. Most acquaintance rapes are power rapes, and because most victims do not fight back, they rarely have external bruises or cuts.

## Anger Rapist

The anger rapist is angry at women in general or at a particular woman. If the victim reminds him of that woman, he is likely to be more violent. It would be a mistake for a victim to use the strategy of saying, "Think how you would feel if someone did this to your mother"; he might be raping because of anger at his mother. Victims usually experience even more violence at the hands of the anger rapist than the power rapist.

## Sadistic Rapist

The sadistic rapist has an urge to torture and mutilate. This type comprises a very small percentage of all rapists, but he is the most dangerous. He will probably rape, torture, mutilate, and kill his victim. The victim of a sadistic rapist should fight back and try to escape no matter how much force the rapist exerts, because the probable alternative is an excruciatingly painful death. It is difficult to know which type a rapist is, but if he is violent from the start you may do best to try to escape even if you have to be violent. Your first priority is to save your life.

Acquaintance rapists rarely fall into the last two categories. Most acquaintance rapes are power rapes, and a power rapist will exert as much force as necessary to overpower his victim. Fighting with a power rapist may result in physical injury.

If a potential acquaintance rape victim thinks her best choice is to try to prevent the rape by self-defense, she should wait until the assailant has let down his guard to escape or to execute a self-defense technique to a sensitive target area. Unfortunately, most women do not know effective techniques or what constitutes a sensitive target area.

A course in self-defense may provide the skills and knowledge for escaping from a rape situation. A woman usually has the element of surprise on her side if she decides to employ self-defense because the assailant is not likely to expect her to know how.

The best strategy against acquaintance rape is to avoid vulnerable situations. A woman can do this by evaluating the risks in her environment and by carefully interpreting verbal and nonverbal cues from her companion. She should make sure in advance that she has a ride home from a party with friends. By having enough money for a cab, she can avoid having to ask her date to drive her home. Since most acquaintance rapes occur in the man's or the woman's home, dorm room, or apartment, it is best not to go with a date alone to any of those places.

Melanie increased her risk of becoming a victim of acquaintance rape by going to Kurt's room. Almost all acquaintance rapes follow a specific pattern. It is important for girls and women to know this pattern and try to interrupt it and stop rape from happening.

## Patterns in Acquaintance Rape

Researcher Py Bateman has identified a three-stage behavior pattern in acquaintance rapes. First, a rapist does something to make a woman feel uncomfortable (for instance, putting his hand on her knee). This is common at parties or bars when the music is so loud that the couple must be very close to hear each other.

If the victim does not clearly object, the rapist proceeds to the second stage, in which he desensitizes the victim to the intrusion by escalating the behavior (moving his hand to her buttocks, for example). She may feel uneasy at this behavior and suggest going outside for "fresh air." The real reason behind her suggestion may be to avoid letting her friends see how forward he is being, or to keep him from being so close to her. Unless she actually tells him that she is uncomfortable with his "roaming hands," he may misinterpret her suggestion as meaning that she wants to be alone with him. The third stage occurs when they are in an isolated place and the rapist insists on intercourse.

The use of alcohol and drugs is often related to incidents of acquaintance rape. Alcohol reduces inhibitions and dulls perceptions so that the woman is less likely to be alert and the man less concerned about what his date wants. In addition, if alcohol is involved in situations where normally moral men experience peer pressure, they are more likely to behave in an immoral way. For example, they may participate in a gang rape under the influence of alcohol, whereas they would condemn such behavior when sober. A woman who avoids or minimizes alcohol consumption is better able to avoid acquaintance rape. She also needs to be aware of her date's alcohol or drug use and to leave if he is high.

# You Are Not Alone

Although exact figures are not available, we can make a fair estimate of the number of stranger or acquaintance rapes in this country each year. The FBI states that about 82,000 rapes are reported to the police each year in the United States. Those are primarily stranger rapes. It is believed that acquaintance rapes are much more frequent. A survey of college women indicated that they had experienced acquaintance rape much more often than stranger rape, but they were more likely to report the stranger rape to the police.

It is not known what percentage of rapes are reported. Those that are reported are like the tip of an iceberg; we don't know how much of the iceberg is below the surface of the water. If only one-tenth of rapes are reported (a conservative estimate), that would mean that almost 1 million rapes occur in the United States each year. However, several researchers have reported that less than one out of 100 acquaintance rapes is reported to law enforcement authorities. That makes rape a highly significant problem that will affect approximately one in four women during their lifetime.

Although any woman is a potential victim of stranger or acquaintance rape, certain types of women are more likely to be targets, while others are better able to avoid rape. That does not mean that there is a set of tried and true methods to keep a woman safe from rape, but there are things women can do to make themselves less vulnerable. In any case, however, a woman does not cause her rape. The person who rapes is the one responsible for it.

## Who Is at Risk?

Rapists are more likely to select victims who do not appear strong, assertive, and able to take care of themselves. Certain characteristics are more common in victims than in nonvictims. These characteristics include personality elements such as being unassertive, lacking confidence in herself, or having low self-esteem. Some women are more vulnerable because they live in cities where crime is more common, or because they go out on dates often. However, the two most significant factors in a woman's likelihood of being raped are the number of men she dates and the man's degree of intoxication. The more men and the greater the intoxication, the higher the degree of risk.

## Females as Victims

Research has shown that women with low self-esteem are more likely to be victims of rape. Other factors are traditional female behaviors determined by sex-role stereotypes, such as a woman's desire to be popular in her peer group, her feeling that she doesn't control her own environment, and her inability to find help following victimization. That does not mean that every woman who possesses these traits will become an acquaintance rape victim, nor that those who don't have these traits are immune.

Nor is it your fault if you have these traits and you are raped. It is never a victim's fault when a crime is committed against him or her. Some people think that if only they had changed they would not have become a victim, and they go on to the still more erroneous conclusion that the rape was therefore their fault.

**Low Self-Esteem**

If you don't feel good about yourself, you may feel that your needs are not as important as the needs of others. That is not true, but if you believe it is, you may not feel able to ask for what you want. Have you ever been in a situation in which someone asked you what movie you wanted to see and you said, "I don't care" when you really did care? Perhaps you thought the other person wanted to see something else and you didn't want to interfere with his fun or seem pushy by asserting your choice.

If you have been in situations in which you don't ask others to stop doing something that you don't like, such as blowing cigarette smoke in your face, it may be because you have low self-esteem and don't consider your needs as important as someone else's. Chapter 13 contains suggestions on how you can work on improving your self-esteem and self-confidence.

**Communication**

The feelings that keep you from insisting on your rights may also keep you from asking a man to stop doing sexual things if you don't like them. If a man you know forces you to have sex, it is acquaintance rape. But if you do not clearly let him know that you don't want to have sex with him, how can he know? It is important to make your wishes known if you expect your partner to honor them.

## Sex-Role Stereotypes

Young women who believe that the best way to interact with men is to be a traditional female (gentle, kind, subtle, sacrificing, flirtatious, and manipulative) are more likely to be raped than assertive young women. Traditional female stereotypes prevent women from being direct and stating or asking for what they want. Many traditional women try to get what they want by manipulating another person, rather than being direct. Let's look at an example of how these behaviors can lead to acquaintance rape.

# Jane

*Jane prided herself on being a "perfect lady," so when Jim finally asked her out she was delighted. She had been wanting to date him for months, but he had not asked her, so she had figured out a way to get him to make the first move. She had her friend Emily tell Jim how wonderful Jane was and that she had just broken up with her boyfriend. Jim finally took the hint and asked Jane if she would like to go to the school football game.*

*At the game they sat with some of his friends, who had brought beer. The more they drank, the louder they got. Jane did not like to drink, but she took a beer at the start of the game to be a "good sport." Jim's friends started insisting that Jane have more beer so she could really "enjoy the game," and they popped beer cans in her direction to spray her with beer. Jane didn't think it was funny, but she did not want to be a downer so she didn't say anything to Jim.*

*After the game, Jim suggested that they get something to eat, and Jane agreed, to get away from his friends. When he asked where she wanted to go, she said she didn't care, anything was all right with her. So he took her to his house. In the kitchen Jim told Jane where everything was, and he went into the living room to put on some music. Jane cooked dinner for the two of them and set the table with candles to make it look more romantic.*

*After dinner he started kissing her. She really enjoyed being close to him, with the music playing and in the candlelight. He began to push her to do sexual things she didn't want to do, and she tried to stop him by saying that she would like a beer. He got them each another beer and came back to continue where he left off. She didn't know what else to try, so she said she wasn't feeling well. He told her to relax, that sex would make her feel better. Finally she told Jim she wanted him to stop, and he got angry. He said that she had been giving him the come-on all day (drinking at the game, telling him she wanted to go out alone with him, agreeing to go to his house, candlelight, asking for more beer). Who did she think she was now, telling him to stop?*

Jane was very confused. All she thought she had done was to try to please him without complaining about his rowdy friends and their drinking. She would have preferred to go out for dinner, but she didn't want to seem pushy.

What if Jim forced her to have sex because he felt it was his right after she had "led him on"? He would have committed rape. But it is also true that Jane's behavior contributed to the confusion of the situation. Jane could have refused the beer during the game, told Jim's friends to stop spraying her with beer, or asked Jim to move with her. She could have insisted on going out for dinner. She could have told Jim earlier in their sexual encounter just how far she was willing to go. Unfortunately, all the things that Jane could have done to stop the rape did not seem traditionally feminine to her. A "lady," in her view, would not do those things.

## Social Status
Imagine that Jim is very popular and Jane almost never dates because she is not popular. She may put up with things she doesn't like because she is afraid to lose him. This may seem like her last chance. Her social status will improve greatly if she goes out with Jim, because any girlfriend of his is considered part of the "in" group. Is she really willing to throw away her newfound status and popularity because he wants her to go further sexually than she wants?

To answer that question, we must go back to self-esteem. If Jane feels good enough about herself not to trade sex for popularity, she will probably risk losing Jim as a boyfriend and tell him to stop forcing her sexually. On the other hand, if having a popular boyfriend is of utmost importance to her, she may be willing to compromise sexually to some degree to keep the relationship. But if Jim wants her to go further than she is willing to go, it is rape.

### Environmental Factors

Jane did not control her environment to increase her safety. If she had wanted to increase the likelihood of being safe sexually, she would not have stayed with his rowdy, drinking friends. She would not have gone to his house. With her beliefs about gender roles, she may have felt that there was no possibility of the kind of environment that would have made her feel safe. After all, she would have had to ask for what she wanted, which was contrary to her stereotypic sex-role behavior patterns.

### Repeat Victimization

If Jane had been a victim of sexual assault before, she may not have known any other way of acting in a sexual situation. The previous sexual assault could have been with another date or with a relative or family friend. If Jane has learned to relate to men as a sexual victim, she may not know how else she can act, or she may feel that she has no right to act any other way. If that is true, Jane needs to learn other patterns of personal interaction. Suggestions for how to do this and how to deal with the other issues that have contributed to Jane's becoming a victim are given in chapter 13.

## Males as Victims

Many of the patterns Jane encountered that contributed to her vulnerability to rape are also present when men are victims of sexual assault. Some male victims have the same personality characteristics as female victims. Low self-esteem, wanting to be a member of a high-status group, not feeling in control of the environment, and previous victimization may all be contributing factors. Again, it is important to remember that a victim is never responsible for the crime; the person who commits the crime is the person who is responsible for it. There are things men can do, however, to make themselves less vulnerable to acquaintance sexual assault by either male or female assailants. For example, being careful about alcohol consumption and about not being in an isolated place with someone more powerful than they are. These suggestions are discussed in detail in chapter 12.

People who commit acquaintance sexual assault and acquaintance rape often look for the "victim type," people who are not assertive, who don't feel good about themselves, and who have few friends.

Few men who are victimized sexually ever report the assault to the police or anyone else. They are often even more embarrassed than female victims because they fear that being a victim of forced sex by a man means that they are homosexual or weak. They may fear ridicule if they have been forced to have sex with a woman, because they think that men should always be ready and willing to have sex. Finally, they often believe that since males are supposed to be strong and powerful, they cannot let anyone know that they have been overpowered. Chapter 14 further discusses males involved in sexual assault and acquaintance rape.

## Acquaintance Rape During the Teen Years

Most rape, and specifically most acquaintance rape, happens between the ages of fifteen and twenty-five. This is the time when young women are most likely to date and therefore are most vulnerable to date rape. Acquaintance rape is not limited to dating situations; it may be committed by friends of the family, employers, friends, past boyfriends, and even husbands.

Acquaintance rape can happen anytime but is most likely during the teen years. This is true partly because many young women lack practice in dealing with sexual encounters. As they grow older, they are more likely to have learned from experience. In addition, because teenagers have more social freedom than their mothers did, young women face pressures in dating situations that their mothers did not have to deal with at such early ages. A fifteen-year-old today may have to deal with the kinds of pressure her mother faced at twenty with more experience and maturity.

There are also very few "rules" for young people to follow today regarding dating, relationships, and sex. Young people receive conflicting messages from parents, peers, the media, and religion. It may be difficult for them to decide what to do sexually and where and how to draw the line, and few reliable sources of such information are available to them. They struggle through their relationships hoping to do the right thing, without knowing what the right thing is or how to accomplish it.

This book is designed to provide teenagers with information on those questions. Several good general books on sexuality for teenagers can be found in the library. You may want to discuss these issues with an adult whom you trust. Parents can be a good resource for some, but not all parents are comfortable or competent in matters of sex, and they are likely to have grown up in more restrictive social settings. Other adults who may be good resources for discussion are relatives, teachers, counselors, youth group leaders, religious representatives, or friends. But even discussion with an informed adult will not always protect you from sexual assault. Each situation is different and may require different strategies and skills.

## Acquaintance Rape in Adulthood

Even adults who have a better understanding of how to avoid acquaintance or date rape may still become victims of sexual assault. Many of the factors in teenage acquaintance rape are also present in adult acquaintance rape.

## Vicki

*Vicki had been married to Bob for more than twenty years and was happy in her role as wife and mother. Both of her children were away at college, and she found herself with little to do with her time and not much to talk about with Bob when he came home from work. Her life had been very busy with the children, but she had not found anything satisfying to fill the void left by their absence.*

*Bob was a successful attorney who sometimes worked late hours preparing cases. At the office he fell in love with a bright new woman attorney. He came home one day and told Vicki that he wanted a divorce because he no longer found her interesting and attractive and had fallen in love with someone else.*

*Vicki was devastated. She believed she derived all*

*her status from being married to a successful attorney. Now she would have no husband, she had no job skills, and she worried that she could not compete with all the young women in the singles scene. But the thought of spending the rest of her life alone was more than she could bear. Vicki had not dated for twenty-five years, and she didn't think she would know how to play the "dating game," nor was she even sure that she wanted to date. She felt hurt, rejected, discouraged, lonely, and angry.*

*Even though she was nervous and worried about dating, and she felt terrible about herself, Vicki decided she had to go out and meet someone so she could begin to feel better. She dated the first man who asked her out, an executive named Michael. She was unsure how she should act, but because he seemed a perfect gentleman, she felt sure he would not do anything he shouldn't.*

*Michael figured that Vicki should be happy to go out with him, and he was looking forward to a great evening ending up in bed. Vicki did not have the same ending in mind, but since she and Michael never discussed the subject, they were not aware of each other's expectations. Michael assumed that because Vicki had been married, sex would be "no big deal." He assumed that because she was a mature woman she had had sex many times in the past, with Bob and others.*

*They went out to dinner and then to Michael's penthouse apartment for a nightcap. Michael insisted on sex, but Vicki protested. Michael assumed that she was just playing hard to get, so he pushed her to have*

*sex, believing that she would thank him the next day.*
*Vicki felt even worse the next day. She felt that she*
*had been raped, and she had.*

Being older does not create immunity to acquaintance rape. Nor does age automatically bring the understanding needed to be effective at avoiding acquaintance rape.

Some of the same factors that make young people vulnerable also increase vulnerability for older people. It was a bad time for Vicki because she was having trouble dealing with her emotions after the divorce. She had low self-esteem and felt that she needed to be involved with an important man to be important herself. She was unassertive and traditionally female in her behavior. All those factors increased her vulnerability, though they do not mean that she in any way caused the rape. She may be more effective in the future if she understands how these factors make her vulnerable and if she works to adjust her behavior and increase her self-confidence.

## Conclusion

It is important to consider rape a community problem. Society as a whole suffers from rape—acquaintance or stranger, violent or not. Women can become frightened of men and fear having relationships with them, and men can become worried for the women in their lives. This leads to untrusting relationships. Those who have been raped and their families suffer from emotional trauma that may interfere with their lives for years. And those who rape may think that it is acceptable to violate others.

Rapists tend to choose people who they think will be easy victims. Therefore, even if 99 percent of the possible victims are trained in rape prevention strategies, rape will not stop because the remaining one percent will still be vulnerable. Major prevention efforts should be made where they belong—on men to stop raping. But as long as men attempt rape, we can all reduce our vulnerability to be raped if we understand what makes a person a likely target.

It is also very important not to assume that adopting the suggestions in this book makes us invulnerable to rape. Rape can happen to anyone at any time. Rape prevention strategies help to decrease the risk, but the risk never disappears entirely. Awareness strategies are also very important for potential assailants, so that they know what constitutes rape.

# Why Does
# It Happen?

No one reason explains acquaintance rape. Unlike stranger rape, most acquaintance rape is not premeditated for the purpose of doing violence to a woman and degrading her. Stranger rape is premeditated rape. Acquaintance rape usually begins as premeditated or planned sex and ends in aggression only if the victim does not comply with the rapist's demands. What is it about our culture that allows some persons to find it acceptable to force their wishes on others?

Forcing someone to have sex is an act of aggression (demanding your wishes without regard for the rights of others) rather than assertiveness (asking for what you want without violating the rights of others).

## Socialization

Neither boys nor girls are taught to be assertive in our culture. Boys are taught to be aggressive and to achieve their goals, often no matter what the cost. Girls are taught to be passive and to put the needs of others before their own. These behavior patterns set up the dynamic for acquaintance rape. For example, if Greg thinks it is manly to have sex on the first date and Rebecca thinks it is feminine to flirt with Greg and tease him, Greg may rape Rebecca because he thinks he should have sex and because he thinks Rebecca wants it. The messages that contribute to this socialization pattern come from families, friends, school, books, television, movies, music—in short, from all around us.

## Female Socialization

Little girls receive messages from the time they are born to act in a certain way. "Ladylike" behavior is being quiet, passive, friendly, nonthreatening, pleasant, giving, caring, generous, neat, gentle, and nonviolent. Girls are taught to concede in arguments and act like the adult women around them. Any child who learned to read by being introduced to Dick, Jane, Sally, Spot, Puff, Mom, and Dad (the characters in the traditional first-grade reader) learned that girls are supposed to cook for, serve, and clean up after boys while the boys sit at the table and are waited on. The messages we received from those readers confirmed what we observed around us: that females are supposed to do things for males and attend to their comfort and their happiness.

Girls see as role models adult women primarily in service occupations such as teaching, nursing, child care, social work, and secretarial work. These career choices reinforce the belief that women should serve and take care of others. In addition, these professions pay much less money than most traditionally male occupations. Most Americans do not believe that "women's work" is as important as men's; therefore, women are not considered as important as men. In some families, the boy is expected to grow up and carry on the family business, but there is no similar expectation for his sister.

The difference between the way boys and girls are treated even extends to the monetary value placed on their lives; for example, a life insurance policy is purchased for a son, but less insurance or none is purchased for a daughter. One of the acquaintance rape victims interviewed for this book explained that her parents bought life insurance for her brother because he was going to take over the family business. They did not buy any for her because she was "just going to get married." She felt much less important than her brother because of that.

These traditional attitudes are changing slowly, but many young men and women still believe that the sexes should behave in traditionally stereotyped ways. Because men and women of all ages go out on dates, these traditional views may be present in many dating situations.

All of these messages and hundreds of others like them reinforce the idea that boys are more important than girls. In addition, many people think that the only way a girl can really be successful in life is to marry and have a family, even if she has a successful career. Boys can be successful if they do well with their career, regardless of their marital status. Often a woman's success is measured by her association with a man, especially a successful man. The reverse is hardly ever true.

Young girls are not encouraged to play roughly or to experience physical trauma as boys are. Thus girls do not get the message that they can fight back, or move on after they have been knocked down, or experienced pain or a black eye after a fistfight. If girls had learned that they could encounter physical injury and still function, more girls and women might realize they have more options than submitting to an attacker. By protecting girls from physical activity that may result in pain, we encourage them to be victims rather than survivors.

Girls are likely to be encouraged by their parents to take dance and gymnastics rather than football and hockey. The traditional female activities do not provide the opportunity to learn how much violent contact one's body can take and still function. Nor do they provide the opportunity for a girl to learn how to incapacitate an attacker. If she doesn't know what target points are most vulnerable, even a properly executed self-defense technique will probably not allow her to get away. Many girls say that they could not hit another person for fear of hurting him. Girls need to know that it is acceptable to hurt a person who is trying to hurt them. Studying martial arts would provide this type of knowledge, but few girls get such training.

Even women who do learn martial arts are generally smaller and weaker than men. They may be able to minimize the power imbalance between men and women by learning self-defense, but the size and strength differences will always exist.

## Male Socialization

A proud dad may buy a hockey stick or a football for an infant boy with the expectation that the boy will grow up and become a sports hero. The boy will encounter a number of physical injuries while learning these sports. He may even be praised for getting into a fight in a hockey or football game because that behavior is "manly." Contact sports develop physical strength and endurance, while also giving young people some understanding of their physical limitations and pain threshold.

Boys also learn from the first-grade reader that they are more important than girls. After all, Dick and Dad do active and interesting things, while Mom, Jane, and Sally prepare meals for them, serve the meals, and clean up after Dick and Dad. Based on real-life experience, children learn that boys can grow up to be President of the United States; girls can't. Until Geraldine Ferraro ran for office in 1984, girls did not even have a chance at being Vice President. These are a few of the messages that set up a date rape dynamic. Some men believe that since they are more important they can do what they want (like force someone to have sex) at the expense of someone less important (like a girl who doesn't want sex). Television, books, magazines, songs, and newspapers continually reinforce the message that it is acceptable for men to force women to have sex.

## Influence of the Media

Television is probably the most popular form of entertainment for young people today. Few current TV shows provide responsible messages about sexuality. Some programs are exceptions to the norm of portraying irresponsible sexual communication patterns. Many shows, however, portray women as not knowing what they want sexually or as manipulating others to get what they want. Rarely are women portrayed as being direct without also being "uppity" and "aggressive" and therefore undesirable. Television implies that women cannot be feminine and sexy as well as assertive and in control of the situation.

Several years ago on the popular soap opera *General Hospital*, Luke raped Laura. Her response was to marry him soon afterward. The message many people got from this situation was that the reason Laura didn't want to have sex with Luke was that she did not know how good he was in bed; once she experienced Luke's sexual expertise, she wanted to marry him so she could have constant access to such a "stud." In fact, there are an average of 12 acts of sexual intercourse every hour on *General Hospital*, many of them forced.

This type of message is not new. It was sent in the epic movie *Gone With the Wind* when Rhett Butler carried Scarlett O'Hara upstairs to the bedroom and raped her. The next morning, she was delighted with herself and Rhett. Although the message is not new, it is dangerous, leading men to conclude that women don't know what they are missing and that if men just push them beyond their sexual limits women will be forever grateful.

This is the height of paternalism: men thinking they know what is best for women. Men are not the only ones who think that way. Some women also believe it, partly because they think that men know more about sex. If a man dictates how a sexual encounter should proceed, a woman may think he must be right and thus may have trouble believing in her own right to stop it.

## Does No Ever Mean Yes?

Whether a woman who says no in a sexual relationship means it depends on the woman and the circumstance. Some women mean no the first time they say it; others don't mean no even after saying it many times. This variation makes it difficult for the woman who means no the first time she says it. Some men become desensitized to the word because so many of the women in their lives don't seem to mean it. If a man persists in sexual advances after a woman has clearly said no, she may feel angry, frustrated, ignored, unimportant, and unheard. She may try to make him hear her or believe her by being more forceful physically (pushing him away). She may even scream, threaten him, try to escape, or resort to physical violence (hitting him) to make her wishes understood. Why should all this be necessary if she clearly says no the first time and means it? Many women do know what they want in a sexual relationship but are treated as if they don't.

Many men are taught to believe that a woman never means what she says about anything, and they may be right in some instances. Girls and women are expected to be polite and not to say rude or hurtful things. For example, if a little girl were served chocolate pudding (which she usually loves) while having dinner at a friend's house, but the pudding tasted chalky, what would be her most likely response? "I don't want to finish this pudding because it doesn't taste good," or "I'm full, and I don't think I can eat any more right now." Or she may eat the pudding anyway. If she chooses the second, polite and typically female response, she is trying to get what she wants (not to eat the pudding) without being direct about her reason. The third response is the most polite of all, but one in which she gives up her wishes completely.

Consider another common pattern: If a woman who is

clearly distraught and upset is asked by an important man in her life, "What is wrong?" she is likely to respond, "Nothing." In reality something is wrong, and he knows it, especially if she is crying, but she tells him verbally that nothing is wrong. The message he receives from that interaction is that he should pay attention to her body language and ignore her verbal message. After all, her verbal message told him that nothing was wrong; only her body language was consistent with his perceptions.

What about women who say no when they really mean yes or maybe in sexual situations? Some young men have told me that to them no means maybe and maybe means yes. When I ask how many times they have to hear no on a date before they believe it, the response ranges from "once" to "7,579."

Some men say that it depends on how she says no. For instance, if she says no and giggles, that implies yes. If she says no forcefully while removing his hand from her body, he may think she means it. But not all men would stop, especially if they think they know what is best for women or if they feel that sex is their right.

A woman who says no when she means yes runs the risk of "crying wolf," so that her partner may not believe her if and when she really means no. After all, she has been conditioning him all evening to disbelieve her verbal messages. How can he know that all the earlier nos really meant yes but the most recent no meant no? Perhaps her accompanying body language should indicate to him that she really means what she says this time. And if he is considerate, reasonable, and views women as his equals, he may stop sexual advances at that point.

But what if Mike and Lori are on a special date? Mike has been fantasizing about this night for weeks, has spent $50 for dinner, and has been reading Lori's nonverbal messages as sexual come-ons. Even if Mike believes that Lori wants to stop, he may feel that he has a right to continue to push for what he wants. He may not be thinking clearly because he has had too much to drink. He may be thinking that because he spent a lot of money, Lori owes him sex. He may think she is a tease; that she sent all those messages that she wanted sex too (going to his place for a "drink," saying she really wants to get to know him better) and now has the nerve to change her mind.

Although Mike thinks these behaviors mean Lori wants to have sex, he may be misinterpreting her nonverbal messages. Mike may have played out this date in his mind and for his buddies as a night of hot, raw sex, and he thinks that anything less would make the evening a failure. Mike may force Lori to have sexual intercourse against her will, thinking that he has a right. He does not think of it as rape because to him rape is something committed by a stranger, in which violence is used, and after which the woman becomes hysterical.

## Sexual Confusion

Lori may be unsure what she really wants sexually, and so may Mike. Both of them have tapes playing in their minds from important people in their lives regarding what they should do sexually, but the two may be quite contradictory.

The message Lori got from her mother was probably, "Good girls don't," or "Don't you ever come home pregnant." Her father's message may have been something like, "I'll kill him." Girlfriends may say "Be careful!" or "It's O.K. if you really love the guy." Her boyfriend may say "Come on, everybody's doing it," or "You would if you really loved me." Religions give the message, "Wait until marriage," or "You should have sex only with the person you marry." The media messages are that "Sex is glamorous," and "Everybody is doing it."

Messages that males get are a little different because a double standard exists for men and women. Men are encouraged to have sex with many women before marriage to become sexually proficient. However, many men still want to marry innocent and sexually inexperienced women. Male messages usually sound more permissive than ones females get. Mother's tape may be, "I don't want to know about what you do." Father's tape may be, "Don't do anything I wouldn't do," or "Don't bring anyone home pregnant." Male peers may say things like , "Be a stud, go out and score, and have a good time," or "If you don't have sex, something is wrong with you." Girlfriends may give mixed messages such as, "I really want to, but I don't think we should."

As you can see, both males and females are receiving conflicting messages from many sources regarding sexual behavior. But young people also have their own ideas, which become confused with all the rest of the sexual messages. Young people may believe that they know what they want to do sexually before the date begins. Once on the date, however, in the "heat of passion," a decision of no intercourse may become increasingly difficult to stick with because of the sensual urges and desires that are normal in healthy people. When people become sexually excited, vaginal lubrication (wetness) in the female and erection in the male result from an involuntary rush of blood into the pelvic region. Since a larger than normal percentage of blood is in the pelvic region, blood is not rushing into the brain to help you make a good, well-reasoned decision. So even if one goes on a date with intentions of a nonsexual evening, his or her body may be contributing to conflicting feelings about sex.

## Personifying the Penis

Some men use their view of their penis as an excuse to have sex. Have you ever heard the expression, "The little head thinks for the big head"? It implies that the penis has a brain. Some people refer to a penis by a proper name other than that of the man it is attached to, for example, George, or Henry, or Horatio, or more recently in the movie *Peggy Sue Got Married* as "Lucky Chuckie." Naming the penis personifies it. This is very dangerous, because the man no longer takes responsibility for what the penis does: "Lucky Chuckie has a mind of his own and made me do it."

People often refer to the penis by other terms because they are uncomfortable using anatomical terms for body parts. Some of the terms are "cute," such as "weewee" or "dingaling"; others are forceful sounding, such as "ramrod"; others are polite, such as "private parts." All of these terms prevent us from discussing the concept of sexuality in an enlightened and direct way. How can we help others understand facts or feelings about something if we refuse to identify clearly what we are talking about? For

59

example, suppose you tried to say something about your elbow and you called it your "pointed joint"? Most people would think you were odd, and many probably would not know what you were talking about.

When my mother was young my grandfather used to refer to her genitals as her "china dishes." This is not a common term for the vagina, but it was understood in their home. Can you imagine what would have happened if my mother had gone on a date and said to her partner, "You can do anything you want as long as you don't touch my china dishes"? Using incorrect terms for body parts can contribute to the misunderstandings that lead to acquaintance and date rape.

## Sexual Decision-Making

To be able to make a good decision in a sexual situation, a person has to know how to make a good decision. Decision-making should be a process of careful reasoning about facts that leads to the best conclusion possible under the circumstances. Unfortunately, many of us make our sexual decisions by default; that is, the decision that was made for us is what occurs, not the decision we made for ourselves, and we are left to rationalize why the decision was a good one. Many of us are quite proficient at rationalizing, but that does not mean that the outcome was best for the situation.

## Rachelle

*Rachelle and Jordan, both sixteen, were on a date. Rachelle had not thought carefully about whether she wanted to have sex with Jordan, or when she wanted to lose her virginity. They got drunk because they went to a party where alcohol was the only beverage being served. On the way home in the car, Jordan pulled off the road to a secluded place and started making sexual advances. Rachelle was too drunk to know what she was doing, but she had not passed out. Jordan had sex with Rachelle, but without her consent because she was too drunk to give consent.*

In this case, Rachelle had sex by default. There had been no previous discussion about whether, when, or under what circumstances they should have sex. If she had made a decision about sexual intercourse with Jordan, she would have considered many things: what they would use for contraception; what she would do if she became pregnant; how her family and friends would react; what if she contracted a sexually transmitted disease such as AIDS or gonorrhea; whether Jordan was the person she wanted to lose her virginity with; the religious implications; the location of the event; how she would feel about herself and Jordan the next day; what would happen if he tried to force her.

Rachelle did not consider any of those things, but she did end up losing her virginity. If she was like most girls her age, she probably rationalized that Jordan loved her. She was "swept off her feet." The relationship is not likely to last, however. If Jordan does not agree that sex means love, he does not expect a long-term relationship. After all, they are both young and have plenty of time to meet and date many people before they settle down.

In most states, the situation between Rachelle and Jordan would be considered rape, because Rachelle, being drunk, was not able to consent. If a woman is under the influence of a substance, such as alcohol or drugs, that diminishes her reasoning ability, if she is asleep, mentally incompetent, or too young to understand what she is consenting to, under some state laws she is considered unable to consent; intercourse that takes place under those circumstances is rape.

## Attitudes About Forced Sex

Some men believe that in certain situations forced sex is permissible. Men's assumptions about their right to sex were studied by Charlene Muehlenhard and Richard McFall in a survey at Texas A&M and Indiana universities; 106 students were asked to respond anonymously regarding acceptability of behaviors in dating situations. Almost all the men said it was all right for a woman to ask a man out. They said he should accept the invitation but that he might view the woman as very promiscuous because she initiated contact.

The subjects were given three descriptions of dating interactions, which varied with respect to which one initiated the date, where the couple went, and who paid. They were then asked whether forced or coerced sex was justified in any circumstances. Men rated intercourse against the woman's wishes as significantly more justifiable when the woman initiated the date, when the man paid, and when the couple went to the man's apartment.

Thus we see that a woman's assertive actions as well as

the passive behaviors discussed above may be interpreted by men as justification for rape. This does not necessarily mean that women should avoid assertive behavior with men, but rather that they should be aware of how assertiveness may be interpreted by some men.

Researchers at the University of California, Los Angeles, asked similar questions of a group of teens. A large percentage (54 percent) of adolescent males responded that forced sex was acceptable if the woman said yes even though she later changed her mind. What if the woman said yes to kissing but no to intercourse? If she was not specific about what she was saying yes to, the man could interpret the yes to mean that sexual intercourse was acceptable.

Almost 40 percent said that forced sex was acceptable if a man had spent a lot of money on a woman. This is the case in almost every dating situation. Men frequently consider it their responsibility to pay for the date, regardless of the cost, and regardless of who initiated the date. A good reason for a woman to pay her share is that the man is less likely to feel that he deserves sex.

More than half of the men questioned believed that a man had a right to sex if she "led him on." But how can we define being "led on"? Is a woman "leading a man on" if she invites him out for a soda, or if she kisses him, or if she invites him to her house for coffee after a date, or if she accepts a drink he buys her in a bar? Do any of these things give him permission to force sex on her? He may think so if he believes such actions are intended to "lead him on."

Over one-third of the men interviewed in the UCLA study believed that forced sex is acceptable if a man is so turned on that he thinks he can't stop. This is a myth about male sexuality. In fact, there is no time in the male sexual response cycle, except for the split second before ejaculation, when he can't stop. He may not want to stop, or he may feel that he can't stop, but if his mother walked in on him during sexual arousal he almost certainly would and could stop. As a matter of fact, he probably would have trouble continuing.

He may have heard about "blue balls," a phenomenon in which the testicles are engorged with blood as a result of prolonged sexual arousal without ejaculation. This phenomenon is uncomfortable, and he may have the idea that unless the pressure is relieved his testicles will explode, resulting in permanent sterility. Both boys and girls learn the myth about "blue balls," but in reality, of course, the testicles do not explode and the discomfort will not cause sterility. The discomfort dissipates quickly if the man ejaculates, or slowly if he does not. If a man does experience this discomfort, he does not need a female to help him alleviate it. Rather than force his partner to have intercourse, he can masturbate, or he can allow the pressure to subside naturally over several hours. The distaste some people feel about masturbating is less of a problem than rape.

## Solution to the Problem

Men must begin to understand that forced or coercive sex is rape even if the woman is a friend or a lover. They must learn to see forced sex for what it is and try to stop it on a personal or societal level. Chapter 15 deals in greater detail with the issue of male responsibility.

Since socialization is responsible for many of the attitudes that allow men to view forced or coercive sex as acceptable, socialization must be changed. Both men and women must be willing to explore the effects of traditional socialization in encouraging rape. College men can use peer influence to condemn, rather than condone, the view of women as conquests. When these men become adults, they can have impact on the socialization of children. Men must try to educate others about the importance of viewing women as equals and of communicating clearly and consistently regarding feelings. Finally, men must know the facts about forced sex to avoid raping, and being arrested for it when they thought they were "doing the woman a favor."

Women must understand the danger of "playing games" on dates, with no meaning maybe or yes. Women can make their lives safer if they understand the ways in which their behavior increases their vulnerability. If a woman is involved in socializing others, it is important for her to give responsible messages about sexual interaction patterns. Women can also use peer influence to condemn irresponsible behavior exhibited by their friends.

It is important to this and future generations that all of us try to change the traditional socialization patterns that contribute to a rape mentality.

# "He Was Drunk."

Alcohol use has traditionally played an important role in the way sexual behavior is viewed by men and women. The double standard has been very important in excusing male behavior regarding coercive or forced sex; for example, "He got so drunk he didn't know what he was doing," or "He got so drunk he couldn't control himself." In contrast, historically women have been held accountable for sexual assault victimization because of their alcohol use; for example, "She got drunk and passed out; what did she expect?"

Alcohol is socially acceptable in America. Even so, victims of sexual assault are often reluctant to admit having been drunk. Victims would probably be even less likely to admit illegal drug use. We don't know much about the relationship between drugs and sexual assault, but there are probably many similarities between the two situations.

A study of 6,000 American college students by M.P. Koss and others[1] examined the students' acquaintance rape and sexual assault experiences. A significant incidence of alcohol-related sexual victimization was reported. Of those cases reported to the police, 50 percent of the female victims and 75 percent of the assailants had been drinking. The figure is probably low because it excludes

---

[1] *Journal of Consulting and Clinical Psychology*, 55(2), 162–170.

women who were too drunk to remember the assault. Victims who were drunk fear that the police will blame them, and they blame themselves for getting into such a dangerous situation. Therefore, alcohol and drugs are probably involved in many more than 75 percent of sexual assaults by acquaintances.

Alcohol also plays a significant role in the sexual victimization of males. A study was made of 2,000 college students from twenty-three colleges in New York state, using self-report recall measures on sexual experiences; 1,000 students were studied in 1989, and 1,000 different students in 1991. Some interesting relationships between sexual assault experiences and alcohol were revealed (Parrot, 1992).

Almost 150 (approximately 20 percent) of both women and men in both years reported having been the victim of an event that meets the legal definition of rape in New York state. For example, subjects were asked, "Did you ever have sexual intercourse when you didn't want to because someone held you down?" and "Have you ever had sexual intercourse with someone when you were unable to consent because you were under the influence of alcohol or drugs?" A yes answer to either question means that the respondent had been raped according to New York state law. When the yes responses to these two questions were eliminated from the 20 percent, only 2.1 percent of the men in 1989 and 1.3 percent of the men in 1991 still reported having been the victim of an experience that meets the legal definition of rape. When the events in which alcohol was determined to have rendered the person incapable of consent were eliminated for women, 6.8

percent of the women in 1989 and 7.7 percent of the women in 1991 still reported having been victims of rape. These findings include only sexual intercourse; other types of forced sexual behavior (such as oral or anal sex) are considered sodomy or deviate sexual intercourse, not rape, in New York state. In addition, women reported forced sodomy experiences more often than men in both years, both when they were drunk and when they were not.

Men seem to experience internal pressure to have sex. They are influenced by the social mandate always to be ready and willing for sex. They may also be concerned about having a sexual conquest to report to their friends the next day. In such cases, they may have sex when they don't want to, but they were not physically forced by another person. However, many women who are victims of forced sex are threatened, held down, or struck by the man to make them comply. So although men and women both report having unwanted sexual intercourse, the type of force involved for each is usually very different.

Several researchers have examined the incidence of sexual victimization experienced by adult males (Muehlenhard and Cook, 1988). According to these studies, 7 to 16 percent of males report sexual assault (including oral and anal sex) based on external force. Some 38 percent of men report having been verbally pressured into unwanted sexual intercourse.

It is remarkable that men reported such a high incidence of sexual victimization. The male incidence was almost identical to that of the women respondents regarding rape involving alcohol use by either the victim or the assailant, and it approached that of females for other

"HE DIDN'T KNOW WHAT HE WAS DOING."

Individuals Reporting Having Experienced Legal Rape, Controlling for Drugs and Alcohol (by Gender)

forced sexual encounters. Alcohol played a major role in the incidence of victimization for both men and women.

## Conclusion

We will not effectively reduce sexual victimization without eliminating the reliance of so many people on alcohol to loosen inhibitions, to have a good time, to be "one of the boys," or just to have something to do. Many young people put on their "beer goggles" as a way to excuse their actions: "I wouldn't have done that if I had been sober, but I had my beer goggles on," or "I got my courage from out of a bottle." Alcohol is often used as an excuse for antisocial or irresponsible behavior. Sexual assault may occur less frequently if people drink responsibly.

# Athletes and Sexual Assault

*"A girl sticks to the team and she supports the team. That's her deal. She wears a T-shirt to the game all the time and she's going to sleep with somebody that night. She's at the bar, and she's there for whoever doesn't find somebody else, basically."* [1]

After Magic Johnson, the Los Angeles Lakers basketball star, announced that he was HIV-positive, he said that he had had sexual encounters with many women, that he enjoyed it, and that it was expected of him. Wilt Chamberlain, also a Lakers star, claimed to have had sex with more than 20,000 women. Sexual promiscuity seems to be considered acceptable, even desirable, for males or male athletes, but not for women. If a woman claimed the same number of partners, she would be considered a slut, or worse. In American culture, men have much more leeway to behave irresponsibly than women, and male athletes often push that leeway to the extreme. This is true not only regarding the number of sexual partners, but also regarding forced sex with acquaintances.

Sports figures are charged with acquaintance rape and sexual assault at a much higher rate than nonathletes.

[1] Benedict, J. R. (1998) *Athletes and Acquaintance Rape.* Thousand Oaks, CA: Sage Publishing.

Sexual abuse by athletes can be found at every level from high school to the professional teams. In 1990, more than fifty athletes were cited in more than fifteen cases across the United States.[2] For example, four high school football players from Glen Ridge, New Jersey, were charged with the gang rape of a mildly retarded teenage girl. A fifteen-year-old wrestler claimed to have been anally gang-raped by teammates at Sunnyside High School, Washington. In 1997, a juvenile court judge blamed Rancho Bernardo High School officials of ignoring a culture of abuse that resulted in a broomstick rape by student athletes. Richie Parker, a Top 25 national prospect as a high school player, was charged with first-degree felony sodomy, but he then plea-bargained to a reduced sentence of felony sex abuse in 1997.

We hear about sexual assault, especially gang rape, much more often at the hands of college athletes. The charges of acquaintance rape and sexual assault also extend into the pros. In the last decade, many cases of sexual assault involving college and professional athletes have received national media attention.

## College Cases

*University of Colorado*—Two football players were charged with rape, acquitted, and left school.
*University of Florida*—A football player was charged with sexual battery for holding a student at knife-point.

---

[2] G. Eskenazi, "Male Athletes and Sexual Assault." *Cosmopolitan*, February 1991.

*University of Minnesota*—Three players were charged with gang rape after a game in Madison, Wisconsin.

*St. John's University*—A woman claimed to have been sexually assaulted by five members of the lacrosse team.

*University of California at Berkeley*—A first-year student claimed to have been gang-raped by four football team members.

*Syracuse University*—A football player, Tom Watson, was charged with criminal counts of rape and sodomy; he pleaded guilty to sexual misconduct. Mike Owens, also a football player, was charged with rape.

*University of Oklahoma*—Nigel Clay, a football player, was sentenced to ten years in prison for acquaintance rape.

## Professional Cases

*Mike Tyson*—former heavyweight boxing champion, was convicted of raping and sodomizing Desiré Washington, a contestant in the Black Miss America Pageant.

*Jim Brown*—football Hall of Famer of the Cleveland Browns, was charged with sexual assault and acquitted.

*Gerald Perry*—Denver Broncos football player, was charged with and acquitted of rape but agreed to counseling.

*Aaron Pryor*—former junior welterweight champion, was charged with committing sexual assault and pleaded no contest to a lesser charge.

*Kevin Allen*—Philadelphia Eagles lineman, was found guilty of rape and sentenced to three years in prison.

*Mossy Cade*—team member of the Green Bay Packers, was convicted of rape.

*Marcus Webb*—team member of the Boston Celtics, was

charged with first-degree felony rape in 1994 and con-victed of third-degree felony rape.

Athletes are disproportionately involved in sexual assault incidents on college campuses. But college ath-letes are not the only group who commit sexual violence. It is not uncommon for us to hear of high-profile cases involving high school, college, and professional athletes who have been charged with and sometimes convicted of many types of sex crimes, including sexual assault,date rape, relationship battering, rape, male and female sodomy, gang rape, and videotaping of sexual assaults. This is very disturbing, and might be prompted by the fact that, "Athletes are taught to react physically, not verbally. They are also used getting their way," according to sports psychologist Harvey Dulberg.[3]

In 1995, 112 college athletes were charged with sexual assault or relationship battering. Most of the victims were other students. While athletes compose about 3 percent of the college population, they account for 19 percent of sex-ual assaults, and 35 percent of the acts of domestic vio-lence.[4] Most of the violators are from high-profile team sports, such as basketball or football.[5] These men are often famous, consider themselves above the law, and are used to getting what they want. Furthermore, they pride them-selves on their physical prowess.

"They say, 'Well, she probably doesn't want to, but I'm so good she's gonna love this.' Because that's what you tell

---

[3] Tim Cornell, *Boston Herald,* June 12, 1997, p. 6.
[4] Benedict, 1996, *New York Times* p. 39, Section A.
[5] Steve Jacobson, *Newsday,* May 13, 1995, St. Louis Post-Dispatch, p. 1C.

yourself. Because you lie to yourself about how good you are in what you do. If you have to go up against Michael Jordan, you're going to tell yourself, 'I can play Michael Jordan.' You have to because the minute you doubt yourself, you're done."[6]

Male athletes are socialized in special ways in today's culture. Top male athletes are looked up to almost as gods, and because of their fame they can sell us anything from aftershave to underwear to sneakers. Their high status and well-defined manhood based on physical achievement may also lead them to believe that they are above the law. They are trained to be aggressive on the field, court, or ice, and many don't know when or how to turn the aggression off when they leave the game. They also may not know how to interpret the signals of female fans. Peer pressure is often involved in the case of acquaintance rape, either because the man believes that he is expected to "report" in the locker room the next day, or because other men encourage him to "do it" (as is often the case in gang rape).

## Gang Rape

Peer pressure, alcohol and drug use, and involvement in all-male groups contribute to the incidence of acquaintance rape, but are crucial elements in gang rape. The male bonding that occurs in teams has been found to contribute to gang rape. Most of the gang rape charges against

------

[6] Benedict, J. R. (1998) *Athletes and Acquaintance Rape.* Thousand Oaks, CA: Sage Publishing.

athletes involve members of contact sports and team sports such as football and basketball rather than players of individual sports such as tennis or golf.[7]

# Alcohol

Alcohol is a significant factor when it comes to acquaintance rape and sexual assault for all men, but especially for athletes. Alcohol can release pent-up aggression, dull one's perceptions, and make one more vulnerable to peer pressure. Most acquaintance rapes by athletes are committed after a game. If the team won, they are out celebrating the victory; if not, they are "drowning their sorrows." In most cases of reported acquaintance rape, the man had been drinking, according to M. P. Koss, C. A. Gidycz, and N. Wisniewski.[8]

# Attributing Blame

Those who subscribe to the "just world" theory believe that rape victims deserve what they get. If a woman was drunk, people say, she deserved to be raped because women shouldn't get drunk. On the other hand, men are often excused for sexual aggression if they have been drinking heavily, because "they can't help themselves," or "boys will be boys."

If the woman assaulted has a bad reputation, whether

[7]Sandler, cited in J. Neimark. "Out of Bounds? The Truth About Athletes and Rape." *Mademoiselle*, May 1991.

[8] *Journal of Consulting and Clinical Psychology*, 55(2), 162–170.

deserved or not, she is more likely to be blamed for the rape. Men who believe in traditional sex roles and male sexual dominance are more likely than others to engage in verbal sexual coercion and forcible rape, according to C. L. Muehlenhard and P. L. Falcon.[9] The extent to which fraternity men and athletes subscribe to these beliefs varies. If they tend to do so, however, they are more likely to consider sexual assault acceptable.

## Aggression

Controlled aggression is an important part of many contact sports. The adrenaline rush that occurs on the field may carry over to post-game activities. Athletes take what they want in an aggressive way off the field much the way they do on the field.[10] The rules that govern behavior on the playing field are different from those of social relationships. And because of socialization, men and women play the "game" of sex by different rules. Men often compare sex with sport by the terms they use describe it: "How far did you get?" "We only got to second base last night, but next time I'll score!"

## Celebrity and Privilege

Athletes are viewed by many people as deserving of special privileges. Coaches and fans often contribute to the players' sense of entitlement. Female fans who express adoration for

---

[9] Sex Roles, 23(5/6), 241–259.
[10] Neimark.

star players are likely targets of sexual assault; a player may find it difficult to distinguish between a fan and a willing sexual partner. Since female fans often pursue sexual encounters with players, some athletes believe that they can have sex with anyone at any time.

High status is associated with an increase in the athlete's risk of committing sexual assault. Special treatment by fans, schools, and alumni can foster a sense of entitlement and exemption from rules. One Big Ten coach phoned a victim of rape by a player and pressured her to drop charges so as not to hurt the player's reputation and the team's ability to win. Another coach explained to a reporter, "I think that if rape is inevitable, [she should] relax and enjoy it."

This does not mean that women should never date athletes, or that all athletes are potential rapists. It does mean, however, that because of their special status and training, athletes may be more likely to be charged with rape. Therefore, coaches need to consider how they can train their athletes to be successful both on and off the field. Male athletes need to learn what behaviors are appropriate in which settings and to act accordingly. Our culture should rethink the way we assign celebrity status to athletes for being aggressive and sometimes violent.

Not all coaches consider rape acceptable and believe that their players are above the law. Many coaches are active in imparting a sense of morality and ethics to their athletes. And decidedly, not all athletes rape. In fact, some team athletes take the lead and look out for their fellow players, teaching them to avoid inappropriate behavior regarding alcohol, sex, and other social situations.

# "Was It Really Rape If She Went Out with Him Again?"

Some people cannot understand how a rape victim could go out with the rapist again. After all, how could she bear to be in the same room with him? There are several explanations.

Some victims have such low self-esteem that they feel they are worthless without a date, that any man is better than no date. The victim may say, "I know what he did to me, but that's all I deserve." Or she may say, "As soon as he gets to know the real me, he will fall in love with me and stop doing that. He will change for me."

She may have watched her father be abusive toward her mother in a similar way and come to believe that is how adult sexual relationships are supposed to be. Or she may have been sexually assaulted as a child and thus knows nothing but forced sexual experiences.

Some victims may not want to believe that someone they love could do anything so terrible to them, so they redefine rape in their minds. That is what Rita did. Rita's rapist was an athlete who had been abusing alcohol.

## Rita

*"We were two totally different people, Rob and I. Because of that, most people were surprised when they heard that we were dating. What could we possibly*

have in common? Rob was your typical jock, and I was the brainy one. Baseball and football were his greatest loves; math and science were mine. Rob would walk through the halls of the school like a king walking through his palace. People looked up to him. I, on the other hand, was content with my group of friends. Sure, they were almost all underclassmen like me, but I would rather have friends respect me than idolize me. Even how we spent time with our friends was different. Rob would usually spend his weekends going to parties or hanging out with friends and drinking, whereas I would stay at home or maybe go to a friend's house to watch a movie.

"Physically, the differences were even more obvious. He was six-two and very muscular. His legs were like tree trunks, and his arms could probably crush me if he held me too hard. On the other hand, I was barely five feet and very petite. My whole hand could almost fit in his palm, and I had to stand on tiptoes to kiss him good-bye.

"Even our attitudes and values were different. He lived life one day at a time, never giving much thought to what tomorrow would bring, whereas I always looked toward tomorrow and all it had to offer. He had been the only boy and the youngest of three children. Therefore, he was used to getting what he wanted. I grew up among seven children, so I learned at an early age to consider the feelings of others. I was sensitive, and I tried to put the needs of other people before my own. In a sense, my biggest problem was that I cared too much.

"Another difference that may not have seemed

*important was our ages. He was seventeen and I was only fourteen. Sure, I was mature for my age, but there are some things that you can only learn in time through experience. I still had no idea what to expect sexually. Having been raised in the Catholic faith, there was only one thing that I knew definitely. I was sure that I did not want to have sex until I was married, and I made that very clear to Rob.*

*"My six-month anniversary with Rob was on Tuesday, September 30. Rob had to work after school, so I would not get to see him. I wasn't really happy about that, but I told myself that I would see him on the weekend. Friday afternoon, when he drove me home from school, I asked him what he wanted to do that night.*

*"'Oh, well, I have to work until eight, and then I was going to go out with Jim and some of my other friends,' he said.*

*"I was confused, 'I thought we were going out tonight,' I replied. 'We didn't have a chance to celebrate our anniversary.'*

*"'Oh yeah, I forgot. I'm sorry,' he said. 'Maybe tomorrow night?'*

*"'Tomorrow night? You promised me on Tuesday that I would get to see you tonight.'*

*"'Well, if you want, you can go out with us,' he suggested. 'Jim's girlfriend and some of her friends will be there, I'm sure.'*

*I really didn't want to go. I was uncomfortable with his friends because they were all older, but I wanted to be with Rob. 'Fine, I'll go with you,' I replied.*

*"I went over to Rob's house at about eight, and his*

friend Chris picked us up shortly afterward. We went to Jim's house. Five of Rob's other friends had already arrived and had started drinking. None of them was female. 'Where is Jessica?' I asked Rob, referring to Jim's girlfriend.

"'Oh, she decided to do something else with her friends tonight,' he replied.

"I stared at him in disbelief. He had brought me there knowing full well that it would only be him and six of his male friends, and that all they were going to do was drink.

"'I feel really uncomfortable,' I said, only loud enough for him to hear.

"'Oh, don't worry about it. Nothing is going to happen,' he said reassuringly.

"I felt I had no choice but to believe him, so I followed him to the kitchen where his friends had started playing quarters, a drinking game. The object is to get your quarter into a central cup. If you succeed, you have someone else drink the contents of the cup. I didn't want to play—I had never drunk before—but Rob insisted. At first, I did fairly well and could often make someone else drink. However, when one of the guys got the quarter in the cup, most of the time he would make me drink. So it was not long before I was drunk. I wasn't in control of my senses, so I decided to lie down for a while. Jim took me to his sister's room, and I collapsed on the bed.

"I vaguely remember hearing the door open. As I turned my head, I saw Rob approach the bed. He sat down beside me and asked how I was feeling. I could barely speak. My head was spinning. He began to rub my back. Slowly, he slid his fingers beneath my shirt. He leaned over to whisper, 'I love you,' in my ear. Before I knew it, he was lying beside me, pressing his chest against my back, and his fingers were wandering farther and farther down my body. He reached around my waist as if to give me a hug, but instead he unbuttoned my jeans. Again he told me how much he loved me, as he slowly slid my jeans off. I was very confused. He had never touched me below the waist before.

"'What are you doing?' I asked, my words slurring together.

"'You make me so happy,' he said, as he pressed up against me. 'That's why I love you so much.' His words were followed by the faint sound of a snap coming undone. 'I want you to make me happy,' he said as he pulled his jeans down.

"'No, please don't,' I begged. 'I told you I don't want to have sex until I'm married.'

"Don't worry, we won't,' he said. 'This is okay.'

"I didn't want to do anything but sleep until he was ready to take me home. However, he had something else in mind. I was lying on my stomach and could barely move. It would have been impossible for me to stop him, and I was too disoriented to realize what was happening until I felt my body being torn in half. He was having anal sex with me.

"I never wanted to believe that Rob would hurt me. He loved me, or at least he said he did. But if he loved me, how could he hurt me that way? How could he totally disregard what I wanted? Those questions were so complex that it was difficult to answer them, so I *ignored them. Instead, I justified his actions. He was drunk, I told myself. He really didn't mean to do it. Technically, he did not have sex with me. I had let him think that it was okay by not stopping him. For my own peace of mind, I had to justify his actions because it was easier to do that than to face the truth.*

*"A few weeks after that dreadful night, I was confronted with a similar situation that became a turning point in my life. I had gone to Rob's house after school and found that his sister was not at home. 'Where is Linda?' I asked.*

*"'Oh, she won't be home until tonight,' he said. 'She has an interview in the city, so we have the house to ourselves. Isn't that great?'*

*"Wonderful, I thought to myself as I headed toward the living room. I did not like the idea of being alone with him, but there was not much I could do about it by then, so I decided to keep busy by starting my homework. However, Rob had other things in mind.*

*"'Why don't you come up to my room and do your homework there?' he said.*

*"'I would rather not,' I said.*

*"'Please,' he said, as he grabbed my arm.*

*"'I'm not going to get any work done if I go up there,' I said. 'You know that.'*

*"'I know,' he said. 'But that's okay, because I didn't want to work anyway. I want to do what we did the other night.'*

*"'No,' I said immediately.*

*"'Why not?' he insisted, pulling me up from the couch.*

*"'Please, Rob, let go. I just don't want to.'*

*"'But why?'*

*"'It hurt. That's why,' I said angrily.*

*"'I promise it won't hurt this time,' he said, as he led me to the stairs.*

*"'I really don't want to, though.'*

*"'Come on, don't you trust me?' he asked, his voice rising with anger.*

*"Of course, I trusted him. He loved me. He would never hurt me. He would not make me do anything I didn't want to do. How could I refuse him? If I did, that would signal that something was wrong. My mind couldn't handle that. I could not deal with the fact that he didn't love me, so I did not argue. It was as horrible as the first time, but I blocked it out. That was all I could do, and I had to repress it to keep my sanity. It was to be three years before I could accept the true meaning of what happened that night.*

*"During the second semester of my freshman year in college, I came home from a chemistry prelim mentally exhausted. I couldn't think long enough to get any work accomplished, so I decided to go to a program on acquaintance rape that was being held in the lounge. The discussion was interesting, but what stuck in my mind was the definition of rape. 'Rape is any form of forced sexual intercourse, whether it is vaginal, anal, or oral,' the speaker said. Her words struck me numb. I had never believed that he had raped me because anal intercourse was not rape. But that was what he did to me, and now I had to face the truth. Somehow I made it back to my room. I sat on my bed and cried for hours. I could no longer ignore the reality of what had happened that night.*

*"For the past two years I have been trying to work through a myriad of painful feelings. I am filled with so much anger and hate. A part of me wants to see Rob suffer so he can at least have a clue as to how I feel. Another part of me wants to forgive him because it is the kind thing to do. However, it is definitely not the easy thing to do. If I knew he were truly sorry for what he did, maybe I could forgive him, but, unfortunately, I don't think he will ever realize how much he hurt me physically and emotionally. What he did to me that one night changed me more drastically than anything else that I have ever experienced. After I broke up with Rob, which I did not do for a year, it was another year before I was able to enter into a relationship again. And even then, it took a great deal of persistence on Michael's part. After two months of his phone calls and flowers, I finally agreed to go out with him.*

*"I was fortunate to find someone the second time who truly cared about me. Michael has been instrumental in the rebuilding of my self-esteem. He has been patient with me when the emotional pain of my memories has caused me to push him away. He has loved me for who I am and not for what I have given him. And he has provided the support I have needed in my efforts to cope with the trauma.*

*"With Michael's support, I was able to confront Rob with my feelings. Two summers ago, Rob called to see how I was doing. It was not unusual for him to call once in a while. He had never wanted me to break up with him, and whenever he got a chance he asked me to reconsider. Usually, I dreaded his calls, but this time*

85

*I was glad, because I was finally ready to tell him exactly how I felt. Rather than telling him on the phone, though, I invited him to come over. It was something that I wanted to do in person.*

*"'As far as I'm concerned, you raped me that night.'*

*"'Please don't use that word,' he said.*

*"I stared at him in disbelief. 'You better believe I am going to use that word,' I said, 'because that is what you did. I know. I have to deal with it every day of my life.'*

*"'I'm sorry. I never meant to hurt you,' he said half-heartedly. 'Please forgive me.'*

*"'How can you be sorry?' I demanded. 'You don't even understand what you have done to me.'*

*"'I know, but please, please try to forgive me.'*

*"'I don't know if that will ever be possible,' I said. 'You don't know what it is like waking up in the middle of the night with recurring nightmares. You haven't seen the look in my boyfriend's eyes when I yell at him to stay away because I'm terrified of being hurt again. You don't know how I feel hurting someone who truly cares about me because you claimed you loved me and hurt me more than you could imagine possible. I don't know if I will ever be able to forgive you for that.'*

*"He was speechless. What could he possibly say? Telling him, however, made me feel a lot better. It made me feel stronger. Still, though, the memories haunt me. I don't know if they will ever go away."*

# Coping with Difficult Emotions

If you have been the victim of acquaintance or date rape, you are probably experiencing many new and confusing feelings. You may be unsure exactly what happened to you and what it will mean to you. Should you tell anyone? If so, whom should you tell? How will they react? Will they believe you? What are you feeling about yourself? What are you feeling about the guy?

What does this mean about you? If you were forced to have sex but flirted with the guy a little, whose fault was it? You may have invited him to your house after the date, or you may have gone to his. You may have been drinking, or you may have been drunk. What if you were wearing a low-cut top or a skirt with a very high slit? Does that mean you were asking for it? The answer is always no! You are not responsible for someone else's actions.

What he did to you was force his penis into your vagina. That is rape. In most states, rape is sexual intercourse against a woman's will and without her consent. In other states, other sexual encounters also constitute rape. In some states, any forced sexual encounter with either a man or a woman is considered rape. Even if you did go to his house or were drunk, if you did not give your consent or if you said no but sexual intercourse occurred, it was rape. Many people in these situations say that they got themselves into a bad situation, or they were taken advantage of. In fact, they were raped.

# The Rape Trauma Syndrome

Most victims of sexual assault experience the rape trauma syndrome. This disorder has several phases: the acute or crisis phase, the disorientation phase, and the reorientation phase.

## Crisis Phase

In the crisis phase, immediately following the rape, victims may be calm (in shock) or upset (angry or guilty), or inappropriately carefree. During this time many victims report feeling powerlessness, fear, anxiety, shame, embarrassment, shock, guilt, depression, and disbelief. This phase may last days or even longer.

## Disorientation Phase

In the disorientation phase, victims are not sure how to act and may have trouble interacting with others. They may try to repress the memory of the rape. Sometimes they change their behavior patterns significantly to avoid future involvement. They may stop dating to avoid situations in which they think acquaintance rape could occur. Since they are not sure why the rape did occur, they may stop doing almost anything outside of home. Fearful that the memory of the rape will be triggered by some event, they limit activities and the number of people with whom they interact.

## Reorientation Phase

In the reorientation phase, the victim feels stronger and has some idea how and why the rape happened. She can begin making constructive changes in her life to regain some control and freedom. She realizes that she will never be able to return to the way things were before the rape, but she can incorporate the rape into her life to make her future something positive. Counseling and the support of a friend or relative help most women to reach this emotionally positive stage. Unfortunately, not all rape victims are able to get to this point. Some try to repress the memory and never move past the disorientation phase.

## What Does Being Raped Mean About You?

If you were a virgin before you were forced to have sex, are you still a virgin? What is virginity? Virginity can be defined physically according to the absence or presence of the hymen (the skin covering the vaginal opening), behaviorally (according to whether you have had sexual intercourse), or emotionally (based on your freely giving yourself sexually to someone else). The presence or absence of the hymen is not a good indicator of virginity. Some women are born without a hymen, and most lose the hymen in nonsexual activities such as riding a bicycle, exercising, inserting a tampon, or having a gynecological exam. In a small number of women, the hymen must be surgically removed because it prevents passage of menstrual flow. Even though these women no longer have a hymen, this does not have any relation to their virginity.

Thus, we need to consider virginity as a behavioral and emotional condition. If you have consensual sexual intercourse, you are not a virgin. But until you do, you still are.

If we define a virgin as a person who has not had consensual sexual intercourse, we can still include victims of date or acquaintance rape in the category of virgin. A victim of rape did not have consensual sexual intercourse; she was a victim of sexual violence. As such, she is still a virgin.

## Rape Does Not Make You "Easy"

The fact that you have had nonconsensual sex once with someone does not obligate you to have sex again with that person or anyone else. In fact, rape does not mean anything about you as a willing sexual partner because you did not decide to have sex. The decision was taken away from you.

Some victims of date rape react by believing that they do not have a right to say no to any other man. This is true especially of victims of date or acquaintance rape who were virgins at the time. These women may have believed that virginity is good, and nonvirginity is bad. Now they believe that they are nonvirgins and consequently are bad. They may think they no longer have the right to put their needs before the needs of others. Some women believe that virginity is the only acceptable reason to refuse sexual intercourse. Once they no longer perceive themselves as virgins, they feel they no longer have an acceptable reason to say no to sex.

In reality, any person has the right at any time to say no to any sexual act, regardless of how many times she or he has had sex before with any partner. She or he even has the right to say no to a partner with whom she or he previously had consensual sex. This is a moral and legal right.

## Being a Rape Victim Does Not Make You a Bad Person

You may also feel that when you have been the victim of acquaintance or date rape you are bad because you have had sex before marriage, or that you now have a reputation for being "loose." Remember that you did not have consensual sex, and therefore you cannot be held accountable for that act of sexual intercourse.

Imagine that you were taking a final exam. Without your consent, the person next to you was copying your answers on his paper. This was something you were involved in, but you did not do so consensually, and therefore you were not at fault. The person who copied your answers was to blame for the wrongdoing. Or imagine that you were walking by yourself and someone grabbed your purse. You were the victim of a crime; therefore, you are not to blame.

You must think of your involvement in date rape in the same way. You were there, and you were involved, but you did not give your consent. You were the victim. Some people will say that you deserved what happened because you had been drinking or you went to his apartment. But they do not say similar things to the person whose paper was copied or the person who was robbed. They do not say, "Well, if you hadn't been sitting in that seat it would not have happened; therefore you deserved it"; nor, "You know New York City is dangerous, you shouldn't have gone there in the first place; but since you did, you deserved to have your purse stolen." But they do make such statements to a victim of date or acquaintance rape, blaming her for her manner of dress, the amount of alcohol she had to drink, being at the place where it happened, and her having had previous sexual experience. Sometimes people say, "What's the big deal? You had sex often enough before." Wouldn't such a statement be ridiculous if it were applied to the robbery victim? "Why are you complaining about being robbed; don't you give money to charities all the time?" In one situation the person is acting voluntarily; in the other the person is being forced. When you are forced, you are not to blame for what occurs; if you are acting voluntarily you are accountable for what happens.

The best way to put such an experience in perspective is to understand your feelings and the feelings of those around you. You need to be prepared for the emotional turmoil that will accompany your telling others about the event. Even though the rape happened to you, your whole family may be very upset and act as if they have been victims.

Other people may treat you as if you are bad, or as if you deserved what happened because of some previous behavior on your part (like going to his apartment). It is important to know that you were not to blame, that you were a victim, and that you are not bad or loose because you were raped. It is also important to try to figure out in advance who will be able and willing to help you and who will blame you. Perhaps most important, you should know your rights and where you can go to get help. These matters are discussed in chapters 11 and 12.

## How Are You Feeling . . .

You are probably experiencing a variety of emotions about yourself and the people around you. You may not believe that it happened, or you may feel numb, angry, embarrassed, or ashamed. You may not be able to understand or explain many of these feelings, but they are there and important for you to deal with.

## . . . About the Person Who Raped You?

How are you feeling about the person who raped you? Remember, he did it to you; you did not do it to yourself, and you did not do it to him. You are probably angry, but you may think your anger is unjustified because you were partly to blame. He raped you, and so he does deserve any anger you are feeling. You may think that because he is a nice man, or because you have known him for a long time, he couldn't have done such a terrible thing to you. After all, nice men don't rape, and so what happened must not have been rape because he is a friend of the family, or your brother's best friend. You may think that someone you cared for so much would not do such a thing to you. It's hard to face the fact that he did not care for you as you did for him.

The fact that you knew him and felt positive about him may keep you from believing that what happened was rape, or that he could have hurt you on purpose. Therefore, you may feel that if he didn't behave inappropriately, it must have been you that did. You may tell yourself that your behavior gave him permission to force you to have sex, and so he was not wrong. So you end up feeling that you deserved everything you got.

## . . . About the World?

When you are able to come to terms with the fact that you were raped by someone you knew and trusted, and perhaps even cared for a great deal, you may question your understanding of the world. You used to think you had good judgment, but maybe you didn't if you chose that man to spend time with; you trusted him, and look what happened.

So now you may be questioning your judgment all the time. What if you go out and you see him or someone who reminds you of him? How can you know what classes to take in school? They might even discuss the topic of rape in class. He or his friends may be in those classes. Some date rape victims worry about every decision they make, fearing that their judgment is so poor that they may make a similar or worse mistake in the future. They stop doing things that require decisions, which means that they pretty much stop doing anything. Trust in personal judgment and in others is gone. This is especially likely to happen if the victim told her family or friends about the rape and they blamed her for it or did not believe her.

### . . . About Your Family?

Your family is who you will probably hope you can turn to for support, but you may not feel that you can tell them. How will they react? Will they blame you? Some families respond better than the victim thought they would; some do not respond as well.

You must decide for yourself whether to tell your family. In general, it is best to tell at least one family member so that you have an ally to help you make decisions and support you during difficult periods. A family member may be able to help you think things through and give advice when decisions are hard for you to make, but the decisions must be yours. Do not do what someone else advises unless it feels like the right thing to do. If you respond in a way that is against your best judgment, you are likely to blame the one who advised you if the outcome is negative.

Regardless of the outcome of your decisions after rape, they must be yours. That does not mean that you shouldn't seek advice and information. But it would be unwise to seek advice from someone who would be disappointed in you if you chose another route. Your adviser must be someone who can and will support you regardless of the decisions you make.

Some families react in a nonsupportive way because they do not know how to be helpful. They may be embarrassed, frightened for you, angry at the situation, angry at you for putting them through it, or they may feel helpless. If this is the way they respond, you must find someone who can give you emotional support. The local Rape Crisis Center has counselors who can help you deal with this crisis. Your parents, friends, or significant other (boyfriend or girlfriend) may also be able to find help there in dealing with the fact that you are a rape victim. With this support, they may become more understanding of your situation and more supportive of you.

## . . . About Your Friends?

Your friends may be good resources for you, and they may be able to help you make good decisions. They are likely to have your best interests at heart without expecting anything from you. It is important for you to know how your friends think about date rape before you turn to them for help.

Some women friends may not be as helpful as you would like. If your friends are like you in many ways, they may sense that if you were the victim of date rape, they also might be vulnerable. For that reason they may not want to believe that you were really raped, or they may believe that you were raped but that it was your fault. A friend with whom you are almost identical in interests, tastes, and behavior may want to believe that you were raped only because you did something to deserve it. Such a friend will not feel so vulnerable because she will think that she can avoid rape by avoiding that behavior.

Another reason such a friend may not be very helpful is that she may have been raped in the past. She may have been trying to forget the rape, and now you are reminding her of it.

Friends may not be helpful in ways you want. They may want you to press charges and have the rapist punished. If you don't want to go to the police, you may feel that you are being coerced again by a "friend." Friends can be most supportive by letting you know that they still feel positively about you and want to help in whatever way you need. The help must be what you want, not what they want, because your regaining control over your life is the only way to recover.

Some men may feel bad that they were not able to protect you from the rape. Some may think that you invited the rape by your actions and therefore may blame you. You do not need people around you who blame you or make you feel guilty. If you are uncomfortable with any of the people who want to help you, you have a right to insist that they leave. A representative from the Rape Crisis

Center may be able to help you assert your rights if you are having trouble doing it by yourself.

You may feel angry at your friends for not believing you and not supporting you. You may think that they should know what you want and how you would respond in a dating situation, since you have discussed these scenarios with them so often. They may be making you feel worse than you already feel. You do not have to listen to them, believe them, or spend time with them! You need to trust yourself and make decisions that you believe are best for you.

The first thing you need to do is heal, and then if you have the energy and interest you can decide how to deal with your anger at your friends.

# Whose Fault Is It?

Many people who are involved in acquaintance rape are unsure where the fault lies. Victims often assume the blame for having done something that they believe contributed to the rape, such as being drunk or going to an isolated place with the rapist. Many assailants don't believe that what they did was rape. They think it was just a sexual situation in which the victim needed a little "push." The assailant often believes that the victim really wanted sex but couldn't acknowledge her desire because she was worried about her reputation. If he pushes her to have sex, even if she says no, he assumes that he is doing her a favor by giving her what she wants.

## The Person Who Rapes Is Responsible

In reality, the person who commits the crime is responsible for it. If the man forced, threatened, used violence, or coerced the woman to have sex, it was rape. It does not matter if the woman has no bruises, if she did not put up a fight, or if she had had sex with him before. Anytime a person is forced to have sex, it is a crime.

Susan Estrich in her book *Real Rape* describes a hypothetical situation in which a person takes your car that is parked in front of your home. The car was unlocked. Was the crime grand larceny? Yes. Would it be grand larceny if you knew the person who took your car? Yes. Would it be grand larceny if you had allowed the person to drive the same car six months ago? Yes. You do not have to fight the person off and come away with bruises to call this a crime. You do not have to warn everyone who admires your car that they may not take it. Your lack of consent is implied. The person who took your car took something from you without your consent.

The same standards should apply to a rape situation. If an assailant "takes" sex from you without your consent and against your will, it is rape. It doesn't matter how well you know the person. You were not asking to have your car stolen because you left it unlocked. Similarly, for instance, women are not asking to be raped because they have been drinking.

## Legal Responses

Although acquaintance rape and date rape are against the law, law enforcement officials often fail to treat incidents of rape for what they are. Police are most likely to believe that you are a victim of rape if you: are a young woman, have bruises or injuries, don't know the assailant, didn't do anything (in their biased view) to "contribute" to the rape, reported the crime to the police immediately, are hysterical immediately following the rape, and have medical evidence collected within a few hours of the rape.

Because of the nature of the crime, many victims do not report to the police at all. If they ever do report the rape, it may be months or years later. Of course, if you don't think that what has happened to you was rape, you will neither report it to the police immediately nor have medical evidence collected. Many women do not identify what has happened to them as rape until an authority on the subject identifies it as rape and against the law.

Even though a woman may not describe what happened to her as rape, she may still feel like a victim. She may be experiencing the rape trauma syndrome. In the first phase of this syndrome, the victim may react hysterically (crying uncontrollably, screaming, not wanting to be touched) or she may be stunned. The stunned reaction may be mistaken by the nonmedical observer as calm. This may lead police and inexperienced medical personnel to believe that she is not having emotional problems. Thus, they may believe that she couldn't be a rape victim, when in fact her response is typical.

Many police officers have difficulty believing a woman who says she has been raped if they believe the rape myths (see chapter 3) and do not understand the patterns of behavior that lead to acquaintance rape. Therefore, many victims of acquaintance rape face being told that their case is unfounded or that there is not enough evidence to present to the district attorney.

Police are also not likely to believe men who have been victims of sexual assault. If a man has been a victim of assault by an acquaintance (forced intercourse, oral sex, or anal sex), he is unlikely to report it to the police. Some men feel that their masculinity is in question if they are overpowered by another man. Some men fear that they may be gay and that that somehow explains why another man would sexually assault them. Male victims of male assailants, as well as police, need to understand that men who force other men to have sex do so not primarily for sexual pleasure, but for domination.

When a man is sexually victimized, it does not, in fact, mean anything about his masculinity. It means that he was sought out as an object of domination. But if a man is worried that he may be a "latent homosexual,"* and his fears are apparently verified by the fact that he was assaulted by another man, he may not want to report the crime for fear that others will believe he is homosexual. If a man believes that rape is something that happens only to women, he begins to question his masculinity.

## Societal Responses

Most people in the United States believe the rape myths and thus are not likely to believe a victim of acquaintance rape.

Most women learn very early that it is not acceptable to fight or to hurt someone, especially someone they care about and trust. Women also learn that it would be fruitless to try to defend themselves against someone bigger and stronger than they are. Many date rapes are committed by someone the victim knows and trusts. She may believe that he will come to his senses at any moment and stop forcing her to have sex. It is a cruel but common distortion to hold a person responsible for an assault committed against him or her. Failing to fight back cannot cause an assault.

---

*The psychological community no longer believes in the concept of latent homosexuality. A person's sexual orientation is established in early childhood. One cannot be "turned" homosexual by engaging in one act of same-sex behavior. However, some less-informed individuals may still believe that latent (potential) homosexuality is possible.

Traditional societal patterns of sexual interaction assign to men the responsibility of initiating all dating and sexual encounters. A woman is expected to control sexual activity, although she is rarely given any specific training in how to do it. A woman must keep her wits about her at all times if she is to control a sexual situation. But she is also expected to cooperate socially and make sure her date is having fun. If a woman drinks what he offers her, she may lose her ability to defend herself. Although she is not forcing him to have intercourse, people often say it is her fault for not stopping it, rather than his fault for pushing her. People are likely to say that a man was so drunk he couldn't control himself, but women are expected to control themselves and their dates whether they are drunk or not.

Although many people think that a man who is drunk cannot control himself sexually, the law does not recognize drunkenness as permission to rape. Thoughtful people put the blame on the man whose actions constitute rape, rather than on the woman who is unable to stop him from raping her.

Another behavior for which a woman is unfairly blamed is going to a man's apartment or inviting him to hers, especially on the first date. Inviting him in for coffee usually means that she is offering him coffee, nothing more. He, however, may interpret it as an invitation to sex. Many who believe the rape myths blame her for being alone with him. After all, they say, she is supposed to control the situation and keep it from getting out of hand sexually. If she ends up in an isolated place and is forced to have sex, people may believe it is her fault for not remaining in a safer environment.

The woman may even be blamed for being a tease and leading the man on. Some insist that there is only one reason for a man and a woman to be alone in an apartment, and that is for sex. So some may believe if she allows herself to be alone with a man, especially on a first date, she is leading him on and deserves whatever she gets. People who believe these ideas blame the victim for something she usually cannot control.

What if a woman has sex with many men? Traditionally, female behavioral virginity is considered desirable before marriage. If you are not a virgin before marriage, you may be thought to be "spoiled goods." Why does it make a difference if you have sex with more than one person? On the other hand, many believe the woman is even more at fault if she has had many partners. For example, some believe that a prostitute cannot be raped; presumably because she has had sex with many men, she has given up her right to say no. In fact, prostitutes can be raped.

Any woman can be raped, no matter how many men she has had as sexual partners. The number of sexual partners is irrelevant, and the relationship she has with the man is also irrelevant. She may even be raped by a man with whom she has had consensual sex in the past. Anytime a woman does not want to have sex but is forced to do so, that act is rape.

Another common myth is that a woman is responsible for a man's sexual excitement, especially if she did something to turn him on. The fact is that we are all responsible for our own sexual excitement. The limbic system of the brain, which controls emotion, turns us on and off sexually. A partner may be the stimulus, but it is our own

brain that turns us on and off. If a woman kisses her partner, even if he becomes sexually excited, he has no right
to conclude that she intends to have intercourse. She may
feel responsible and think she should have intercourse
with him if he becomes sexually excited in response to her
stimulation. But she is under no obligation to do this.

What if a woman says no but the man doesn't believe
she means it? Should she have to say it more than once?
Some men don't acknowledge that a woman ever means
no. Others need to have the no accompanied by a con-
vincing and specific action to believe it. In other words, if
you say no but giggle or let him continue to unbutton your
blouse, he is less likely to pay attention to your no. Does
this give him the right to force sex? No! However, he may
think that you really want sex because your body language is different from your verbal message. He also may
not hear your no if he has been drinking or if he feels that
he has a right to sex because you "led him on."

Some young women acquire a reputation for being sexually promiscuous. If a man believes that you have had sex
with every other man on the basketball team but you won't
sleep with him, he may feel angry and rejected. If he forces
you to have sex under those circumstances, it is rape. He may
feel justified, however, and others may condone his behavior
even though no one has the right to force sex on anyone.

## Safety Decreases with Increased Vulnerability

Some things that women do can increase their vulnerability to sexual assault. Although it is never a woman's fault

if she is raped, there are ways in which she can increase her safety. Whether or not you have used any prevention strategy, you are not to blame if rape occurs. But because it is in your interest to decrease your vulnerability, you may want to think about the suggestions that follow.

If you were raped, you may have done something that your friends or your own brain call stupid, something that in retrospect you wish you hadn't done. If this is so, you should identify the behavior and avoid it under similar circumstances in the future. Does this mean that you cannot ever kiss a man again, or have a drink? No. What it means is that because some of your actions may decrease your reasoning ability, or be incorrectly interpreted by others, you need to increase your safety in these situations.

For instance, if you are at a party with a girlfriend who drove and you don't know any other people there, make sure you know where your friend is and when she is leaving. Don't be left behind and have to count on someone you just met to take you home. He could rape you in his car.

Remember several important points about your behavior at a party:

- Don't get so drunk that you can't keep track of your friend's whereabouts (she may be drinking too).

- Don't go to a secluded place with someone you have just met.

- Always have cab or bus fare in the event that your ride does leave without you, and be aware of how late public transportation is available.

- Don't rely on someone you have just met to give you a ride.

Suppose you are at a party and you want to be alone with someone, perhaps because there is too much noise to talk. Be sure to tell the friend you came with that you are going to another room, how long you expect to be there, and the name of the person you will be with. For example, you may say, "Jane, I am going upstairs with Jim Ellis to see his room. We will be there for about fifteen minutes. Please come and get me if you are ready to go before I come down." That way Jim knows that you plan to spend only a short time alone with him, and your friend knows where to find you. This is a good strategy if you feel you must go to his room, but it would be much better to refuse to go to a secluded place with someone you don't know well.

It is important to remember that acquaintance rape or date rape sometimes happens when people have just met each other, but sometimes the assailant has known the victim for years. He may be your teacher, or your boss, or your friend. If you are with someone who begins to become "too familiar" (does suggestive or sexual things that make you uncomfortable), it may be a sign that he will go too far if he has the opportunity. Thus the same principles apply to people you have known for some time, even someone you may have been dating, as well as to people you have just met.

What if you are kissing your date and really enjoying it, and then he starts to "fool around." You may enjoy that too but not be sure you should be doing it; so you make a feeble attempt to say no, but you don't sound as if you mean it because you actually are not sure you want to stop. He doesn't stop. He goes on to try to unbutton your pants. You have been telling him no without meaning it for the last half hour, but now you really want him to stop. This time you say no more forcefully, but he still thinks you mean yes, so he continues. By telling him no without meaning it, you encourage him to believe that your no means yes. It is important to say what you mean. If you are not sure, tell him that you don't know what you want but that he should believe that no means no when you say it.

Let's say you want to take a man to your apartment to "fool around" with him, but you don't want to have intercourse. What can you do? First you should tell him what your limits are. Don't take him to an empty apartment. Be sure your roommates are there. If you have asked them to come if you call for help, they may be able to help you to control the situation.

These are some examples of how a woman's behavior may contribute to her safety. Many more suggestions are offered in chapter 13. But remember, no matter what behaviors you engage in, you are never responsible for a crime that someone else commits against you.

It is important to understand where the blame and responsibility lie for acquaintance rape and sexual assault. The fact that the person you are with misinterprets your behavior and believes that you want sex does not give him the right to force you to have sex. No one has that right.

You may encounter people who say that you can cause rape by your behavior. They are wrong. They may also diminish the importance of rape by saying that sex is just sex and no big deal if you have had sex before. They do not understand the causes of rape or the devastating effects it can have on the victim.

Some friends may tell you that forced sex with a date is not as serious as stranger rape when a maniac jumps out of the bushes and rapes you brutally. That is wrong! Both stranger rape and acquaintance rape are emotionally difficult for the victim. Stranger rape may be more traumatic physically, but acquaintance rape is often more traumatic emotionally, partly because a woman may no longer feel able to trust her own judgment. She may not be able to trust men anymore. She may not have the support and understanding of friends and family that would be likely in a case of stranger rape. And the police are even less likely to believe her.

# Whom Should You Tell?

If you have been raped by an acquaintance, you are probably wondering what you should do. Decision-making may be harder now than usual. Who will believe you? Who will say it was your fault? What if you are pregnant? How will you know if you have contracted a sexually transmitted disease? What should you do if you want to press charges and have him arrested? Where can you go for emotional help and support?

These are all important questions. Unfortunately, few people know much about acquaintance rape, and even fewer will be able to give you good advice. If you find people who know about acquaintance rape, how will you know if they can help you?

You may think that your friends and family are the best people to tell because they care about you and will help you to make good decisions. That may be true, but they will also have their own emotions about your having been raped, which may prevent them from giving you the kind of help you need.

## Friends

The friends you may want to tell could be female or male. You may be thinking about telling your boyfriend or your best girlfriend or your roommates. These people may be supportive, but they may also have trouble dealing with your discomfort and pain and the reality of the fact that you were raped.

## Kim

*Kim was very religious and wanted to be a virgin when she married. She and Scott had been going together for three years, since their junior year in high school. They went away to different colleges and saw each other on weekends about once a month. In between they did not date other people, though they both made new friends and acquaintances.*

*Kim was working on a small group project with John, a guy in her sociology class, which required them to meet several times out of class. The fourth time they met was in Kim's dorm room. Her roommate was there too, but was having trouble concentrating on her studying with Kim and John talking, so she went to the library.*

*Once they were alone, John began to make sexual advances, which Kim resisted. She explained that she and Scott were dating and planned to marry after they graduated from college. John told her that she should experience other guys before she settled down with her high school sweetheart. She said that that was her decision and she did not want to date other guys. John said he knew she wanted it (meaning sex) because of the signals she was giving him when they were together working on the project. John forced Kim to have intercourse with him, ignoring her vehement protests.*

*John left immediately after he had finished, and*

*Kim lay crying on her bed. She did not know what to do, so she called Scott, thinking that he would be able to comfort her and tell her what to do. To her surprise, Scott became very quiet and told her he needed time to think about things. He was hurt, disappointed, and confused. He decided to consult the priest on campus, but he was even more confused after talking to the chaplain.*

*It was important to Scott that he marry a virgin. Kim was no longer a virgin in his eyes. And even though the priest said that the rape was not Kim's fault, Scott could not help but question why she had invited John to her room to study. He also believed that a woman should fight back to prevent a rape, and Kim didn't.*

*Although he still loved Kim, he could not bring himself to trust her or believe her. She was no longer the one he wanted to marry. Their relationship ended a few months later when Scott told Kim that he could only marry a virgin.*

Even though Scott and Kim had a good relationship before the rape, Scott was not able to be helpful to Kim afterward. He had his own emotional problems to deal with. He knew very little about rape, and he blamed Kim for not being able to avoid it. His response was not only not helpful to Kim, it was harmful, because he added to her emotional burden. Although she was not to blame, she felt that she should have been able to avoid the rape and so blamed herself for not being stronger.

Kim needed the support of someone who knew enough about acquaintance rape to help her stop blaming herself and get the emotional and medical help that she needed.

She also needed someone to help her decide whom to tell and how to tell them. In addition, she needed advice about her legal rights and what she should do regarding John. She did not want to see him again, but they were in the same sociology class. Scott was not able to give her any of this help, and he needed emotional help himself.

Feelings of guilt prevent many victims from telling others about the rape. Few acquaintance rape victims tell their parents immediately (although some do years later), but many tell their friends or siblings that they have had a "bad" sexual experience. It appears that the response of the first person who is told determines how the victim feels about the event in the future.

## Bonita

*Bonita was manager of the football team and really enjoyed the close friendships she had developed with many of the players, but she hadn't dated any of them.*

*One night Bonita was asleep in bed when one of the players showed up at her apartment to see her. Her roommates told him that she was sleeping, but he convinced them that he was a good friend and she would be happy to see him. So they let him into her room.*

*Once in the room, he climbed on the bed with Bonita and started kissing her. She was startled when awakened and did not know what was happening. Once she realized who he was, he was pulling the covers off. Bonita could smell alcohol on his breath and thought he was drunk. She asked what he wanted, and he said, "You know." Bonita didn't want to have sex with him, but she was afraid to tell him to stop because she thought he would hurt her.*

*Since he was drunk, it took him a long time to ejaculate, and he was hurting Bonita with his clumsy attempts at intercourse. Bonita was crying through the entire rape. When he finally came, he passed out on top of her and didn't wake up for several hours. Once he came to, he got dressed and left.*

*Bonita staggered into her roommates' room and asked them how he had gotten in. When they said they had let him in, Bonita was furious and said, "You let him in to rape me!" Their response was that it couldn't have been rape. She had been interested in having a relationship with him ever since she met him, so what was she complaining about?*

*Bonita was devastated. She had been raped, and her best friends said that she was to blame.*

Not all friends respond in negative ways when they are told about an acquaintance rape. But a person must be mature and know quite a bit about acquaintance rape to be helpful. Frequently it is better to seek help from older people who are informed about the topic. Parents, teachers, counselors, clergy, rape crisis counselors, doctors, or nurses may be helpful, but not all adults in those categories will be able to help. They may also have trouble dealing with their own emotional response to the rape, or they may not know enough about acquaintance rape to be good sources of support.

## Family
Parents often say that they feel as if the whole family had been violated when one of their children is raped.

This makes the victim feel that her very personal problems are being ignored. Some parents are able to put their feelings aside long enough to be helpful; others try to deny their feelings; and still others are too upset to be helpful at all.

## Annette

*When Annette was a junior in high school, she accepted a ride home from school from a man, who subsequently raped her. She had met the man through a mutual friend and was surprised to see him waiting for her after school one day. He offered her a ride, and she gladly accepted, especially because all her friends had seen him in his sports car. He told her he wanted to take her home by the "scenic route." Several miles from her house, he stopped the car in a remote park area and forced her to have intercourse. Then he drove her home.*

*When she got in the house, her mother started scolding her because she was late. She told her mother what had happened, but her mother screamed that she was a sinner and needed to be saved. Her mother said she deserved what she got for accepting a ride with a man none of them knew, and she should be ashamed for bringing disgrace upon the family.*

Annette's mother was too distraught by her own feelings to be able to help Annette. She caused more problems for Annette by blaming her for the rape.

Before you tell a family member, you need to assess

how that person will be likely to react to your rape. It should be someone who has been able to help you in other situations, who is concerned about you, and who wants you to be able to deal with whatever problems you have. Remember that you are the most important person right now. Don't confide in people or ask them for help just because you think their feelings would be hurt if you didn't ask.

## Tiffany

*Tiffany was raped by a date when she was in high school. She was very upset and wanted to tell someone, but she was worried about how her family would deal with the aftermath of rape. She was afraid that her brother would do something stupid, like beating up or even killing the guy. She thought her mother would be a good support person, but she did not want the entire family to know.*

*When she told her mother about the rape and her fears about her brother, her mother was very supportive. She helped Tiffany figure out how to get help without letting her brother know right away.*

*Several years later, when Tiffany had healed fairly well from the emotional trauma of the rape, she told her brother about it. He was older and less hotheaded and was able to deal with his anger and frustration in a constructive way by being supportive to Tiffany. Her assailant had moved out of the community by then, so Tiffany didn't have to worry about her brother possibly running into him and doing something for which he could be arrested or put in jail.*

Tiffany's mother was helpful, but her brother would not have been if she had told him immediately after the rape. She made a wise choice to keep it from him at that time. Telling him about the rape would only have added to her worries rather than diminishing them.

Some family members may have very good intentions but turn out not to be the best people to help you. In one case, a mother whose daughter confided in her immediately after the rape went to the college and took over the decision-making because the daughter did not feel able to make decisions for herself. The attorneys representing the college suggested that the mother retain legal representation for her daughter and suggested a local attorney. The mother was grateful for the advice and did hire that attorney. Unfortunately, he knew nothing about acquaintance rape and seemed to have the college's welfare in mind rather than the victim's. As a result, the case was handled quietly and the victim's wishes were ignored. She wanted the assailant removed from campus so she would not have to see him during her daily routine. On the contrary, the assailant was allowed to remain on campus, the victim dropped out of school, and the college received minimal negative publicity.

If the mother had not been so emotionally involved herself, she might have realized that it was not wise to hire an attorney recommended by the college. It is difficult for people who are emotionally involved with a victim of rape to think clearly. In a case like this, a professional such as a rape crisis counselor and a trusted family member or friend may be a good combination of support for one who has been raped.

## Rape Crisis Centers

Rape crisis counselors know from experience which attorneys, medical personnel, and therapists are qualified and able to be helpful in specific cases. They can also work with all members of the family or friends who are involved.

If you call a Rape Crisis Center, you will talk with a highly trained counselor over the phone. You do not have to identify yourself, so you can talk for a while to see if you feel comfortable with him or her. If so, you may ask the counselor to meet you at your home, the hospital, or any other place to decide what to do next. The counselor will not tell you what to do but will advise you of your options. The decision-making is up to you, and a good counselor will support you in whatever you decide.

Rape crisis counselors are generally the most specialized counselors available to you, and rape crisis services are free. These counselors will work with you as long as you need it, advising you on legal issues, going to the hospital or to court with you, and helping you to return to a normal life. Although counselors in Rape Crisis Centers are well trained and empathetic, an individual counselor may not be the right one for you. If you are not having a positive experience with any counselor, you should change counselors.

## Other Counselors

Therapists, medical personnel, and religious counselors all may be able to help after a rape, but not all are trained specifically in rape counseling. Even fewer are educated about acquaintance rape issues.

117

## Therapists

The therapist who may be helpful to you may come from almost any group of professionally trained and recognized therapists. Many victims prefer to talk to a female therapist rather than a male therapist, but just because a therapist is female does not make her the right person for you. Some male therapists may be helpful in dealing with the aftermath of rape. If you are already seeing a therapist about other matters and have a good relationship with that person, you may want to discuss the rape with him or her.

On the other hand, if he or she is not familiar with acquaintance rape issues or makes you feel uncomfortable, you may want to seek out someone who is more able to assist you in this area. If your therapist does not know much about acquaintance rape, you may suggest that he or she contact the Rape Crisis Center. You may also want to recommend the book *The Rape Victim: Clinical and Community Approaches to Treatment* by M. Koss and M. Harvey.[1]

You can find a therapist who knows about acquaintance rape by calling your local Rape Crisis Center and asking for a list of recommended therapists. It would be best to get several names, so that if you don't hit it off with the first person, you have other options. Therapists listed in the Yellow Pages under sex therapy are not necessarily familiar with this issue. Select your therapist carefully, and do not continue with one who blames you for the rape or makes you feel guilty.

---

[1] Lexington, MA: Stephen Greene Press, 1987.

## Medical Personnel

There are several sources for the immediate medical help you will need after rape, but the best is probably the emergency room of a hospital that has a special rape trauma team. This group of medical professionals may have a different title in your hospital, but such a team will be able to meet your needs much better than those untrained in sexual assault. The team will probably consist of a doctor, a nurse, a social worker, and perhaps a police officer. They will work to treat all your medical and emotional problems. They will be aware of your needs and be able to discover and treat injuries, even those that are difficult to observe such as inside the vagina. They will also collect specimens in such a way that evidence will be admissible in court if you decide to have the assailant charged with rape.

If there is a chance that you will accuse your assailant legally, you need physical evidence collected by medically qualified personnel as soon after the rape as possible, at least within twelve hours. You should not do anything that could destroy evidence, such as washing your face or any part of your body, combing your hair, changing your clothes, brushing your teeth, gargling, or douching. Although wanting to cleanse your body to remove all evidence of the rape is a common emotional need after being violated, those actions destroy physical evidence.

If you decide to proceed legally but were not examined and do not have medical evidence, your opportunity is not necessarily lost. In many cases of acquaintance rape, the assailant admits that sexual intercourse occurred. The case will rest on whether the intercourse was forced or consensual.

Medical professionals who may be helpful to you include doctors, nurses, nurse practitioners, physician's assistants, and medical social workers. You can receive adequate help from any of these people only if you feel comfortable with them, if they understand acquaintance rape issues, and if they are experienced in evidence collection and treatment of victims. These people can help with your physical needs, and they should also consider your emotional needs.

You may need extended emotional counseling that will cost significant amounts of money, as will the help you receive from trained therapists. Such long-term counseling will help you regain normal relationships in your personal life and is different from the crisis counseling you receive immediately after the rape.

## Religious Counselors

These professionals are likely to help you free of charge if counseling is part of their ministry. The same criteria apply as with the other professionals regarding their potential helpfulness. You should feel comfortable with them, they should understand acquaintance rape issues, and they should have training in counseling. These people may be clerical or lay counselors of your religion or of a religious organization.

Regardless of whom you choose to confide in, it is important that they be truly helpful to you. You should feel free to change counselors or stop going to anyone who you feel is not being helpful. You must do whatever you need to do to regain a normal life.

## The Police

You may choose to utilize the legal system after an acquaintance rape. Most victims do not, for a variety of reasons. Perhaps they do not want their private life exposed to the world with little chance of obtaining a conviction. Perhaps they feel guilty about what they see as their contribution to the rape. Perhaps they do not want to be responsible for ruining the assailant's life. Perhaps it was weeks or months before they were willing to admit they were raped.

Reporting rape to law enforcement officials is the focus of the next chapter; however, use of officers or investigators as counselors is discussed here. Some law enforcement officials are specifically trained in stranger and acquaintance rape issues. These officers, who are usually but not always female, may be helpful in informing you of your legal rights. They may tell you that because of the low conviction rate obtained by the district attorney in your community, there is a slim chance of obtaining a conviction if you decide to press charges. They may be able to direct you to medical professionals or therapists. They may just be available to listen to you and give you suggestions for making your environment safer. You may want to develop a friendly relationship with the officer so that you will have someone to call if you want reassurance or if you are in danger in the future.

In any event, the final decision is yours whether to press charges. If you do, the police officer will take your statement, collect evidence, and turn the information over to the district attorney. The quality and quantity of the evidence will help the district attorney decide if the case should be sent to the grand jury, so you should provide as much evidence as possible. In addition to the information the police officer obtains from you, physical and medical evidence will make your case stronger. Seeking medical help immediately after a rape may be helpful for that reason and also be important for your long-term physical well-being.

## Medical Care

You should seek medical care after being raped by a stranger or an acquaintance because you may have been injured internally. There may be tears of the vaginal or rectal tissue, depending on the activity you were forced to perform. In addition, you may become pregnant or you may have contracted a sexually transmitted disease. Therefore, even if you decide not to press charges, you should receive medical care for your own health. If you decide later that you want to press charges, the evidence will be available, and the police and the prosecutor are more likely to believe you if medical evidence was collected.

## Physical Trauma and Pregnancy Prevention

If you do go for medical care, you can be treated within seventy-two hours to prevent pregnancy and at any time for sexually transmitted diseases. The sooner the better, however, especially if there are internal injuries that require treatment. Pregnancy is not a common outcome of rape, but it occasionally occurs. You may wish to ask for the "morning after" pill (RU486) to prevent pregnancy, but you should find out about possible side effects before you accept a prescription. Decisions about pregnancy may also be made if and when pregnancy is confirmed.

## Sexually Transmitted Disease Prevention

Treatment for sexually transmitted diseases (STDs) usually includes an antibiotic at the time of the first visit and several follow-up visits to make sure that a disease has not developed weeks or months after the rape. The follow-up visits are important because some STDs have long incubation periods and may not be detectable within the first few weeks after the rape. Since anyone can have a sexually transmitted disease, you are not immune even if the person who raped you was rich, handsome, or intelligent. As a matter of fact, since those who commit acquaintance rape are often promiscuous, he is probably at high risk for having an STD.

# What Are Your
# Rights?

Acquaintance rape and date rape are against the law. All rape is against the law, but the law has not been applied consistently. There are two ways to proceed under the law as an acquaintance rape victim: You may seek criminal prosecution or file a civil suit. Information on the difference between the two is given later in the chapter.

Victims, assailants, the general public, and the law tend to consider acquaintance rape as being less significant than stranger rape. The degree of violence and force used, a prior relationship with the assailant, and the degree of post-rape hysteria are common but erroneous criteria used to determine whether rape occurred and how it should be treated legally. The victim's sexual history and her socioeconomic status are other factors in erroneous judgments about a rape victim's credibility.

## What Is the Law?

Legal statutes regarding rape vary from state to state. In some states, rape is defined as forced intercourse committed by a man on a woman. Other states have much broader definitions: Either sex can be either the victim or the assailant, and forced sex acts other than sexual intercourse are covered. Some states do not mention the crime of rape in statutes but use more general terms such as sexual assault or sexual abuse. In about half of the states, a woman cannot legally charge her husband with rape. The laws that exclude marital rape were written in the past when a woman was considered the property of her husband, and he could have sex with his wife anytime he wanted. In many states the term rape may not be used if the victim is male; under the law a rape victim may only be female. In those states, sex forced on a man is considered sexual assault.

In many states an act is considered rape or sexual assault if it is against the woman's will and without her consent. A woman has not consented if she says no or if she is drunk or unconscious, asleep, too young to know what she is consenting to, or mentally incompetent. A man who decides that a woman is "asking for it" by being drunk, and thinks he has a right to sex if she has passed out, may find himself charged with rape.

Because state laws differ so greatly, you must check the laws of your state to see what is considered rape or sexual assault. You can find out by contacting a local police agency, a chapter of the National Organization for Women, a Rape Crisis Center, the district attorney's office, an attorney, or a pro-bono legal clinic (free legal services offered by most law schools and by lawyers in most cities).

If you have been sexually assaulted or raped, you should know exactly where the violation falls within the law. You may have, in fact, been raped; but if you are married to the assailant, the act may not be against the law where you live. Similarly, if you are a male victim of forced oral or anal sex, the attack may not be considered rape, but it may be considered sodomy or sexual assault. In some places, the law states that a woman need only be in fear for her safety or her life for a sexual encounter to be considered rape.

Some people refer to "victim-precipitated" rape, meaning that the woman was partially to blame, or "asked for it." Legal distinctions are often drawn between "simple" rape and "aggravated" rape. Simple rape is one in which there is no evidence of violence, threats, or a struggle. This is often the case when the victim and assailant know each other. Aggravated rape is one in which a weapon, a threat, violence, or force is used or there is more than one assailant. Members of the legal community are less likely to accept simple rape for prosecution than aggravated rape. This does not mean that simple rape is not a crime, but fewer people view it as a crime, and it is more difficult to prove in court.

## Diana

*Diana had known Brad for several months, and they had friends in common. After having attended a play with their friends, Brad asked Diana to have a late supper with him. He was really "turned on" by her sexy dress and wanted to get to know her better. She was also interested in getting to know Brad, having been attracted to him for months.*

*They went to a quiet little Italian restaurant, where they shared two bottles of wine and talked for hours. Diana invited Brad to her house for a nightcap. After several drinks, Brad suggested that he give her a hot oil back rub. It sounded wonderful to her, so she agreed to undress and wrap herself in a towel. Brad told her she had nothing to worry about, because he was a minister's son and had only honorable intentions.*

*Halfway through the back rub, Brad started kissing her neck, which felt very sensuous. They enjoyed kissing and fooling around for almost an hour. Suddenly Brad became forceful and told Diana to remove the towel completely. She resisted seriously until Brad grabbed her arms roughly and raised his voice.*

*Diana was very frightened. She knew no one would hear her if she screamed because she was alone for the weekend in a secluded house. Brad forced her to have oral sex and intercourse. Diana did not resist; she remained still, almost as if dead, throughout. She felt as if she were across the room watching the rape. She couldn't believe it was happening to her.*

*After Brad left, she locked the door, took a long, hot shower, and went to bed. She couldn't sleep the entire night. The next day her roommates came home and found her acting like a zombie. They knew something was wrong, but Diana wouldn't tell them what had happened until after hours of questioning. They then persuaded her to go to the police to report the rape.*

*At the police station, she was questioned by a uniformed male officer who insisted that she describe all the details of her dress, how much she had had to drink, and what had happened. He seemed to enjoy the details of the sexual encounter. When he had finished taking the report, he told Diana to take his advice and go home and forget all about it. "You really expect me to believe that you didn't want it after you invited him to your place and you undressed willingly? What did you expect him to do, play cards? The district attorney would laugh at me if I presented this case to him. Do yourself a favor, don't take any more men home!"*

This officer probably didn't believe that what had happened was really rape, but in any case he thought she deserved the attack for "leading him on." No one who has been sexually assaulted is responsible for it, but many people think that certain behavior gives a rapist permission. Although more and more police, district attorneys, and judges understand that there is no such thing as "victim precipitation," many still believe there is.

## What Can You Expect from the Legal System?

You will deal with a number of people and organizations if you go to the police. First, you may contact the police or an attorney to determine what the laws are in your state. You may contact the police to report the crime (so that they have a description of the attacker and his pattern of behavior), even if you do not want to press charges. If you do want to press charges, you will have to talk with a uniformed officer and a detective or an investigator, so that they can gather evidence pertinent to the case. In a criminal proceeding, the district attorney will then become involved to determine if there is enough evidence to seek an indictment from the grand jury. If an indictment is handed down, the case will go to court. You will be confronted by the prosecuting attorney, the defense attorney, the jury, and the judge during the trial.

Most acquaintance rape cases are not reported to the police. Of those that are reported, very few end up in court.

## Will They Prosecute My Case?

The police may feel that there is not enough evidence to turn the case over to the district attorney, or they may feel that it was victim-precipitated rape, implying that you were as much to blame as the rapist. If the case does reach the district attorney, it may still be dropped at that point as not being strong enough for an indictment.

Of the acquaintance rape cases that actually go to trial, few result in conviction. This is because juries are made up of people who believe many of the rape myths discussed in chapter 3. In addition, members of the jury may have been in similar situations in which sex was forced, but they did not consider it rape. Men are understandably reluctant to define someone else's behavior as rape if they have done the same thing and do not consider themselves rapists. Women on juries may be hard on an acquaintance rape victim, wanting to dissociate themselves from such vulnerability and finding it easier to blame the victim.

In some cases, the jury members are in agreement that sexual intercourse occurred but disagree over the issue of consent. If the jury is not convinced beyond a reasonable doubt that the woman was forced, they are reluctant to convict the man for a "misunderstanding."

Many rape victims choose to interact with the legal

system by informing themselves about the law and getting advice as to the wisdom of seeking prosecution. You may want to ask if there is a specially trained rape task force representative, who is more likely to be understanding. You may also want to ask for a female officer.

Judith Rowland, a former assistant district attorney, has written the book *The Ultimate Violation,*[1] in which she describes her experiences in attempting to obtain convictions in acquaintance rape cases. She succeeded in one case by using expert witnesses to demonstrate the rape trauma syndrome. She had therapists and psychiatrists examine the victim and testify that she had experienced the syndrome immediately after the rape, contrasted to her emotional condition before the rape, which was normal. The jury concluded that the forced sex she experienced was rape. The rape trauma syndrome is described in chapter 9.

## Criminal Cases

If you seek criminal prosecution and the district attorney takes your case, the law acts as if the rapist had violated the members of your community by breaking the community law. The case becomes the people of your state vs. the rapist. You become only a witness for the state. The district attorney may not take your case if he or she believes that it is weak or that no crime was committed. If you are successful in a criminal case, the assailant is found guilty. He may receive a suspended sentence or probation, be required to do community service, or be imprisoned.

---

[1] New York: Doubleday and Company, 1985.

130

Unfortunately, the likelihood of a guilty verdict in an acquaintance rape case is very small. If you seek criminal prosecution and lose, you may feel more out of control and helpless than before the trial. You should be aware that your personal life and morality may be described in detail and put into question in the courtroom. You may be verbally intimidated by the rapist's attorney.

Most states have laws to protect the victim from having her entire sexual history revealed in court. These laws are called rape shield laws. Generally, they allow only sexual information related to the case being tried to be revealed in court. An assailant's past criminal record may not be presented in court even if he has been convicted of a similar crime. These legal provisions are made to avoid prejudicing the jury.

The rape shield laws do help protect both the victim and the assailant. If the victim knew that her past sexual history would be revealed, it might keep her from going to court. Similarly, if the assailant's record were revealed in court and he had raped before, the jury might convict him based on his record, not on the merits of the case. So the laws are designed to provide a fair and impartial trial, and they usually work.

## Civil Cases

Because it is so difficult to obtain a criminal conviction, some acquaintance rape victims turn to the civil courts. Criminal conviction requires unanimous decision by the jury that they have been convinced "beyond a reasonable doubt" that the defendant committed the crime. Often in a civil court only a majority of the jurors have to be convinced that the defendant is guilty, but that depends on where the case is heard. If the victim wins or settles out of court, she usually receives a financial award.

In a civil case, the victim is suing the assailant personally. The state is not involved. The victim retains an attorney, who usually charges a percentage of the award the victim receives, usually about 30 percent. The major difference between a civil and a criminal case is the standard of proof required. In a civil case one need only prove a "preponderance of probability," rather than "beyond a reasonable doubt" as in a criminal case. With the same evidence, it is usually easier to win a civil suit than a criminal suit.

A victim may choose to sue someone other than the assailant, charging failure to provide her with protection, especially if the assailant has no money. For example, suppose a woman broke up with her boyfriend, but he refused to return the key to her apartment. She asked the landlord to change the lock but he didn't, and the former boyfriend let himself in and raped her. Such a victim may sue the landlord, claiming that his negligence caused the attack.

If an eighteen-year-old college woman gets drunk at a school function and is raped while she is passed out, she may sue the institution for failing to provide a safe, alcohol-free environment or for failing to prevent alcohol consumption by minors.

## What About Medical and Therapy Costs?

In many places, if you press charges and the case goes to court, you may be eligible for compensation for the costs of medical expenses. The district attorney's office will pay for the medical expenses related to evidence collection. Any costs you may have for emotional or psychological therapy do not fall into that category unless you need a psychiatric evaluation for medical evidence. Long-term therapy costs are not covered.

If you decide not to seek prosecution, you may be able to recover costs by applying to the crime victims' compensation board in your community. Unfortunately, not all communities have such boards. Since the medical costs can be high (initial hospital costs, follow-up medical tests, therapy, etc.), it makes good sense to apply for such help if it is available.

If you decide to seek criminal prosecution, you will not have legal costs because the district attorney represents the state (and you).

It is important to remember that each case is different, and the situation and the evidence in your case may make it easy to win. If violence was involved, you probably will have an easier time in court.

# Protecting Yourself from Rape

There are a number of things you can do to help keep yourself from becoming a victim of acquaintance rape. These strategies and suggestions apply to persons who have never been victims as well as those who have. They are also appropriate to help men become less vulnerable to sexual assault.

Let's focus on potential victims. You can work to prevent acquaintance rape on two levels. First, you can make yourself safer. Second, you can make the world safer for others.

## Things You Can Do for Yourself

### Feel Good About Yourself

If you do not feel good about yourself, you probably don't think you have a right to ask others to stop doing things they want to do that affect you. For example, if you are with a partner who wants sexual intercourse and you only want to kiss, you might assume that your partner has a greater right to his wishes. If you had high self-esteem, you would not feel this way or that you had to stay with someone who wanted you to do things against your wishes.

### Get Emotional Help

Feeling good about yourself may be easier said than done. If you do not feel good about yourself, you must first identify the reasons you are feeling bad before you can do anything to correct the situation. For example, if you feel bad about the fact that you have been raped, perhaps professional counseling may help you to feel better. But you may also be able to gain the same benefits by talking to a sympathetic friend. Pick a friend who will support rather than blame you.

## Stay Away from Those Who Treat You Badly

If you do not like the way others are treating you, one strategy is to tell them what it is about their behavior that makes you uncomfortable, how it makes you feel, and how you would like them to change it. This is called an "I" message. For example, suppose a friend makes fun of the way you wear your hair. You could say, "When you make fun of my hair (offensive behavior), I feel hurt and embarrassed (feelings). I would like you to stop commenting on my hair or help me to change my hairstyle so that we both like it (change message)."

Another possibility is for you to change the thing you are being teased about. Still another possibility is to change friends and surround yourself with people who will be nicer to you. This is not always possible, but perhaps you can minimize the amount of time you spend with people who make you uncomfortable.

No matter what is making you feel bad about yourself, there are people and groups in your community that can help you: school counselors, rape crisis counselors, crisis hotlines, departments of social services, drug or alcohol programs, weight control centers, physical fitness centers, and many others. You can find many of them in the Yellow

Pages of the phone book, or by calling a crisis hotline, which will have referral phone numbers for many of the services you may need. Remember, the best way to feel better about yourself is to find out what is making you feel bad and then to try and deal with it.

## Know You Have a Right to Be Respected

You have a right to be respected and to have your wishes respected. If you want to go to a specific place or to do something in particular on a date, you should be able to do those things unless they are in conflict with the wishes of the other person or are immoral or illegal. An immoral behavior would be doing something wrong such as not telling your date if you have a sexually transmitted disease (such as herpes) before sex. If the other person wants to do something different, the two of you should negotiate, compromise, or at least agree on the activity and location of the date. If your date is not willing to take your wishes seriously or to compromise, he has only his interests in mind. He is not interested in you or your welfare. If you are with someone who does not seem to be interested in your welfare, stop spending time with him!

## Be Careful About Alcohol

Alcohol is frequently present in acquaintance rape situations. Alcohol dulls the senses and impairs your ability to assess situations. It may make you oblivious to the increasing danger of a situation. For example, you may not be aware that your ride has left the party and that you have no way to get home. Or you may mistakenly presume that you are strong enough physically to stop someone from forcing you to have sex. In addition, alcohol decreases inhibitions and may change your date's perceptions so that he thinks he should respond to your refusal in a macho manner and force you to do what he wants.

People often use drinking as an excuse for bad behavior. If you are with a man who is drunk, he may say that he couldn't help himself because the alcohol clouded his judgment and he got "carried away." People sometimes say that a woman who was raped deserved it because she was drunk. Thus, alcohol is sometimes used to excuse men and to blame women for rape, and used by women to blame themselves for the situation.

## Mean What You Say and Say What You Mean

Often, women and men do not really mean what they say. Women are brought up to be nice and try to please everyone. Men are taught to take charge. Therefore, women are afraid to make an angry statement for fear that it may hurt or annoy others, especially a man who feels he should be in charge. So women often try to say difficult things in a nice way, deny their feelings, or not say anything at all.

For example, if a woman feels that a man is getting too intimate on the dance floor, she will probably not tell him how she feels. If he asks her if something is wrong, she may say, "No, it's getting hot in here; let's go outside and cool off." She is denying her feelings and trying to reject his advances in a nice way. However, this nice way may get her into serious trouble, especially if he misinterprets her wanting to "cool off" as wanting to go outside to be more intimate. She needs to learn to reject the behavior, not the person. A more honest and assertive response to the situation would be, "Yes, I am uncomfortable with your kissing my neck, but I would like to keep on dancing if you'll stop it."

Take the example of a woman who is clearly upset, and a man in her life asks what is wrong. She answers, "Nothing!" but her body language more accurately reflects her feelings than do her words. She may mean that she is too upset to talk about it, or perhaps he is the one who upset her and she will not give him the satisfaction of knowing it. The message he receives is that maybe he can trust her body language, but not her words.

Men often do the same thing. If a man is upset, punching walls or crying, and an important woman in his life asks what is wrong, his response is likely to be "Nothing!" But he doesn't really mean nothing. He is likely to feel that he is not supposed to express emotion by crying; that if he talks about the problem he may start to cry. So he doesn't admit that there is a problem. The woman also learns that his words are not as reliable as his body language.

If men and women continue to say one thing in words and another with body language, their partners will not rely on words to understand what is really going on. It would be far more effective for each of us to be honest about our feelings. We would be much more likely to get what we really want without relying on our partners to guess what that is.

**Give Clear Messages**

It's not possible to tell your partner what you want sexually if you don't know yourself. You receive many conflicting messages in your life about sex. Your parents probably tell you something different from the males your age, and that message is probably different from what you hear from your female peers, from the media, and from your religion.

These messages may be confusing, and to make matters worse your heart, your head, and your genitals may all be giving you conflicting messages. It is very important to think about what you want sexually, sort out the conflicts, and try to communicate your resolution(s) clearly to your partner before both of you are feeling the urgency of sexual arousal or the relaxation of inhibitions that accompanies alcohol consumption.

When you have decided what you want sexually, you must communicate it clearly, giving the same message with your words as with your body language. If you really don't want to have sex with him, don't tell him that you just want to be friends while you let him unbutton your blouse. Don't tell him that you don't want to have sex because you have no means of birth control; he may have a condom (rubber) in his wallet. If you don't want to have sex, make that clear with time parameters such as, "I don't go to bed on the first date," or "I want to wait until marriage." If you say, "I don't want to have sex right now," he may think that five minutes later will be all right.

## Avoid Dangerous Situations

The best way to avoid acquaintance rape is to keep out of situations that could become dangerous. It is not always easy to know which situations will be safe and which will not, but some general rules may help. Because they are general rules, it is important to remember that not all the situations described will actually be dangerous, and some that are not mentioned may be dangerous. Factors that are often associated with acquaintance rape include but are not limited to:

- Alcohol and drug use

- Being isolated with a man

- Being with a man in a place where he is under a great deal of peer pressure

- Being with a man who exploits or ignores you

- Being with a man who exhibits antisocial behavior

- Not having your own transportation

- Feeling that your personal space is being violated

The degree of intoxication of a man is the one most important factor in determining whether acquaintance rape will occur. Don't stay with a man who is drunk. If yourself are intoxicated, you will be less able to assess your situation and less effective in making your wishes known.

Being isolated with a man eliminates the possibility of getting help. There may be no one to hear you if you call out. In addition, he may assume that your going with him to an isolated place means that you want to be intimate sexually. If he thinks that is what you intended, he may try to push you to have sex because in his mind, "you really want it" or "you asked for it."

Some men who are kind and considerate when they are alone with a woman are coerced into doing unacceptable things when they are with others who pressure them. This factor is important in gang rape. Imagine a situation in which a group of fraternity men are trying to top each other's male prowess. They see who can drink more, who can lift more weights, and who can pick up women most quickly. If they are really drunk, they may even discuss who has had sex with the most women. If a woman at a party is considered promiscuous, and she is also drunk, they may try to prove who is the "best man" by having sex with her. Some of the brothers may not want to participate but fear being made fun of or labeled gay or impotent. They may simply fear not being considered "one of the boys." Under these circumstances, an otherwise nice man may participate in gang rape.

Men who exploit others in nonsexual situations are more likely to exploit women in sexual situations. If you know someone who asks you to clean his room (just because you are a female), or who leaves you alone at a party where he knows many of the people and you know few, be careful around him in sexual situations. Such men believe that women are less valuable than men and that it is acceptable to treat them as sex objects. He may be the type who strikes a woman when he is angry or who thinks that a woman should meet his sexual desires regardless of her own.

Men who behave antisocially in nonsexual situations are also likely to force women to have sex. For example, men who drive drunk or break other laws are behaving in antisocial ways. Such people frequently do not exhibit regard for others in sexual situations either. If they want sex and their partner does not, they are likely to force sex.

If you do not have your own transportation home from a party or game, you are dependent on your date. If he should start to show signs that you consider dangerous, it is important that you be able to leave without relying on him. Have money to call your parents or for bus or cab fare, or go with a friend who will be willing to drive you when you want to leave.

One of the earliest signs that a situation is becoming dangerous is for a man to invade your personal space and not back off when you tell him he is too close. Personal space is the imaginary boundary that surrounds each of us, the distance from another person that we need to make us feel safe and comfortable. At a party, for example, a man starts to handle your necklace. This makes you uncomfortable, and you take the necklace out of his hand and back up. Your discomfort tells you he is too close.

If a stranger comes into an almost empty movie theater and sits in the seat next to you, that is an invasion of your personal space. The boundary varies with different people. A friend sitting next to you would not make you uncomfortable. Your mother can come very close without your feeling violated, but your school principal must stay farther away for you to feel comfortable.

Early in a relationship you have a wider personal space than you do after you have been dating for a year. If a date begins to violate your personal space, you must let him know that this is unacceptable. If he continues to stay too close, it is a sure sign that he is not taking your wishes into account. This is the universal first stage of acquaintance rape.

## Have a Way Out

What can you do if you are in your own home with a man who you feel may try to force you to have sex? Walk out and leave him there if you sense danger and he won't leave. Go to a safe place, like a neighbor's home, where you can call the police to have him removed.

But what if you fear he won't let you leave through the front door? You should have an escape plan, another way out, like the back door or a window. Most acquaintance rapes take place in the victim's or the assailant's home. If he means to rape you and you leave, he may get angry and trash your house, but that is preferable to being raped. After all, the items in your home are replaceable. Your mental and physical health is not so easily restored.

# Know How to Use Your Weapons

You can use your mind, your voice, and your body as weapons.

## Your Mind

The first way to use your mind is to assess the potential danger of a situation and avoid involvement. The second is to get out of a situation that has become frightening. The third is to get out of a situation in which you think you are in imminent danger.

In the first situation, imagine that David, a macho man whom you do not know well, suggests that you ride with him in his car instead of on the bus provided for a ski trip. David has a reputation for being "fast." Your instincts tell you that many hours in a car with him would put you in a vulnerable situation. You would have virtually no control over events because he is much stronger than you. If you decide not to go with him but to take the bus, you have probably made a wise decision. Even though you are attracted to him, you will have ample opportunity to get to know him better on the slopes, where many other people are around.

In the second case, suppose you are at a fraternity party and a friend introduces you to Tony, a delightful man whom you are enjoying. You dance for most of the evening. When things begin to slow down, he invites you to his room to see his new stereo. In his room you start to kiss and fool around, but at times he tries to push you further than you want to go sexually. He is pretty drunk and is honoring your protests less and less, and you are becoming increasingly uneasy. Just then someone knocks at the door asking to borrow one of his tapes. At that point you say, "It is getting late and I really must be getting home," and you leave the room while someone else is there for protection.

## Your Voice

In both of those scenarios, you used your mind to assess the potential for danger and made a decision to get out of the situation before anything dangerous actually happened. But what if you do not assess the situation as dangerous and you find that you are being forced to do something you don't want to do sexually? What if you cannot just leave to avoid the danger? How can you use your voice as a weapon?

Many women feel embarrassed to raise their voice or scream because they have been taught that it is not ladylike. It is hard to confront someone directly and demand your rights, especially if you are with someone you like and with whom you want to develop a relationship.

The principles you must apply in such situations are these:

- It is better to be embarrassed than raped.

- Yelling may seem unladylike, but it may keep you safe.

- When women yell, men are more likely to take them seriously.

- Yelling when there is no one around to hear you is less effective than yelling where others can hear you.

Imagine being on a picnic in a quiet park with Kevin, whom you have dated just a few times. You are enjoying the afternoon sun, nature, and each other's company. Just when you thought things were going well, he begins to get very insistent about having sex "in a natural setting." You tell him that you don't want to have sex with him in any setting, but he doesn't seem to care. Finally in desperation you yell, "I don't want to have sex with you; if you force me, it is rape." He is likely to stop because he doesn't think of himself as a rapist. If he doesn't stop, however, it may be because he doesn't think you will tell anyone and no one else is around to hear you yell. Thus, yelling may stop him because you startled him by what you said and how you said it; on the other hand, it may not work because you are in a secluded place where no one will hear you.

Suppose your employer calls you into his office and starts to make sexual advances. You have heard that he has done this with other people, and you don't want to have sex with him. There are people in the outer office who will hear if you scream. He doesn't stop when you tell him to, so you yell, "Leave me alone, I don't want this." He does stop then because he fears what the others outside may think, but you are worried about his firing you because you wouldn't have sex with him. If he fires you for that reason, he has broken the law. You could take him to court for sexual harassment and unlawful dismissal. However, you may just decide that no job is worth having to deal with sexual coercion. In either case, you used your voice effectively as a weapon.

## Your Body

In the event that neither of the previous strategies works, you may need to use a physical self-defense maneuver to get to a safe place. Self-defense is difficult for some women to learn because it is contrary to much female socialization. If you have been told all your life not to hurt others, and certainly not to hurt them physically, it may be hard for you to execute a technique if the need arises.

To be effective in employing self-defense, you need to know the vulnerable target areas on the body (such as eyes, knees, ribs, neck, nose, instep), your effective weapons against the body (such as fists, feet, elbows, head), and how to strike effective blows with those weapons. The best way to learn is to take a self-defense course, preferably one designed for women. Then you must practice the techniques consistently to be effective when necessary. A good book on the subject is *Fear or Freedom—A Woman's Options in Social Survival and Physical Defense* by Susan Smith.[1]

---

[1] Racine, WI: Mother Courage Press, 1986.

146

## Know About Rapists

The most important thing to know about rapists, especially those who commit date or acquaintance rape, is that they usually seem normal, just like "any other man." Although some would argue that any man who could rape has psychological problems, he may not appear to be psychologically ill. In other words, you can't tell by looking at someone or even by talking with him if he is a rapist. Those who rape come from all socioeconomic backgrounds and may be found in any occupation. Contrary to sex-role conditioning, a woman can't expect every man she goes out with to want to protect her.

Many men who commit acquaintance rape do not plan rape; they plan sex. That is to say, they plan to have sex at the end of the date, and if the woman does not comply, they push her. Such a man seldom thinks he has done anything wrong, much less raped anyone. In fact, he may even say that the woman was asking for sex by inviting him to her house or by dancing seductively. He may believe that he was doing her a favor by giving her what she wanted without her having to take the responsibility for initiating sex. He may say that he didn't want to have intercourse with her but thought she wanted it and so he obliged.

The more you know about rape and rape prevention, the more you can avoid becoming involved in such situations. You will also know the options if you or someone you know is raped. If you understand the common emotional responses to rape, you may be better able to deal with them.

# Ways to Make Things Safer in the Future

Rape is hard to deal with if you've been victimized. You will need emotional help from a strong support system to be able to cope with the emotional reactions that follow rape. You may also be able to help others who have been raped because you possess a special awareness of the subject. You can use that understanding in the aftermath of rape to help others.

### Volunteer at a Rape Crisis Center

Although not all of the good volunteers at Rape Crisis Centers have been raped, if you have been a victim you possess a special understanding of rape. You may be very effective at helping others because you understand what they have been through.

Volunteering to help others will be effective only if you have worked through the emotional turmoil surrounding your own rape. Once you have done that, the experience may be helpful in two ways. First, you will be helping others who need support and not blame. Second, you are likely to regain a sense of the power and control over your life that you used to feel.

### Work to Change the Law

In most states acquaintance rape and date rape are illegal, although they do not often end in conviction in the criminal justice system. In some states, however, these acts are not actually violations because of flaws in the law. For example, in about half the states women cannot charge their husbands with rape. Also, significant discretion is allowed to law enforcement officials to decide if a rape charge will stand up in court. If they are not sure of the evidence, they are not likely to proceed with the case.

Laws can be changed to eliminate this discretion so that if a rape victim wants to press charges she may do so. Some states are considering laws that would require investigation of every incident of acquaintance rape reported on a college campus. Other changes being considered in some states include establishing marital rape as a crime, creating gender-neutral laws allowing for either males or females to be victims or assailants, and assimilating rape law into assault law. The latter would eliminate the introduction of sexual history, eliminate the marital rape exception, do away with the high age of consent, and reduce the penalties for rape, meaning that more assailants would be convicted if the potential sentence were shorter.

If you would like to see justice in acquaintance rape situations, you may provide input to lawmakers to change the laws so they will more effectively reflect the needs of society today. You may do so by writing to state and local representatives, visiting them, and voting against those who do not treat the issue with the seriousness it deserves.

## Attempt to Prosecute Your Rapist

Since many rapists repeat the offense many times, it is possible that your assailant has raped others and will continue to do so. If you choose to prosecute your rapist and he is convicted, the world may be safer in several ways. First, he will not have access to women while he is in prison. Second, in prison he may have access to a treatment program for sex offenders. Third, just by prosecuting you make clear to him that what he did was wrong; you make him answer for his actions and call his character into question.

### Educate Others About Rape

The more people know about rape, the less likely they are to blame the victim. If an acquaintance rape is reported to them, they will be better able to be supportive to the victim and help her through the trauma. In addition, they are likely to provide correct information regarding evidence collection and reporting procedures. For instance, they can inform the victim that she does not have to press charges or make a decision about going to court immediately, but that early reporting to the police will make her case stronger if she does decide to go to court. If she never goes to court, the information she provides to the police may tell them more about this rapist and his patterns of behavior.

Informing others about rape will help to dispel some of the rape myths. The better informed people are, the better jurors they will be if they have to serve in a rape case. If jurors better understand rape, they will probably bring in more convictions in acquaintance rape cases, possibly resulting in a decrease of incidence. If the court system gives the message that acquaintance rape will be punished, perhaps fewer men will commit the crime.

### Work for Improvement of Services

If you have been through a medical or legal examination following rape, you may have been one of the lucky ones who had a good experience. But you may have had a very bad experience if the professionals working with you were not well trained, or if they believed the rape myths. You have special expertise that could help medical and law enforcement agencies to improve services for rape victims.

Medical personnel should be trained in the use of the rape kit used to collect medical evidence. In addition, medical facilities should have a rape team of sensitive professionals who have streamlined the procedures so that the victim does not have to retell (and in doing so, relive) the details of the rape many times. Members of the rape team should include a female (if possible) physician, nurse practitioner, or physician's assistant to collect the evidence (a male may seem threatening to the victim); a nurse; a social worker; a Rape Crisis Center volunteer; and a well-trained police officer. Each of these people has a specific job to do; they are all important to the team. A special private place should be available for the victim to wait in the hospital, rather than in the middle of the busy waiting area of the emergency room.

Police agencies should train staff members about acquaintance rape and also provide a private place for questioning in the police station. It is very difficult for a victim to recount graphic details of rape with other people listening.

## Work to Change Policies at Your School

If you are at a college, university, or boarding high school, the institution probably has policies to deal with violations of the law or of acceptable social behavior. If the administrators or campus police are not educated about acquaintance rape, they may fail to treat it as a crime; instead, they may blame the victim. Therefore, it is important that they understand the crime and its consequences.

When a woman has been a victim of acquaintance rape, she frequently does not want to see the assailant again. If they go to the same school they will probably see each other on campus, which can be devastating for the victim. She often chooses to leave the school rather than have to see him daily. The institution should act swiftly in these cases to protect her psychological well-being; she should be given the choice of who is to be moved.

A judicial hearing should be held as soon as possible. It should be a private rather than a public hearing because many women faced with having to describe the attack in public refuse to testify. A timely hearing is also in the man's best interest; if he is found not guilty, his name is cleared. The institution also needs to make counseling services available to both victim and assailant.

## Help Develop Community Programs

The best thing you can do for others is to help them avoid rape. Community education programs can help you do this. Effective rape prevention programs frequently include a self-defense component.

You have information about rape that many other people don't have, but you probably don't feel equipped to conduct rape awareness and prevention programs yourself. You may find support in Rape Crisis Centers, at the YWCA or YMCA, among local martial arts instructors, at counseling centers, in police agencies, in hospitals, in women's centers, at colleges and universities, and in men's groups. You may be helpful in a number of ways, depending on your skill level, but perhaps your most important role would be as a communicator of what would have been helpful.

## Conclusion

Many suggestions and strategies in this chapter have been offered to make your world safer from rape. Some of the suggestions may work for you, but others may seem impossible. Don't feel that you have to adopt or learn any of the strategies. However, the more you incorporate into your life, the better protected you will be.

Nevertheless, it is important not to think you are invulnerable to rape once you have incorporated some of these suggestions into your life. These are tools to make you safer, not absolutely safe. The most important thing you can do is never let down your guard. The more aware you are in all situations, the more you increase your safety. The more risks you eliminate, the less you will have to worry in the future.

You may find that you can do only a few of these things now. That's all right too. You may find that you are ready to try more and more as time goes on. Keep updating your rape prevention strategies. You may want to reread this chapter periodically to see what new strategies you want to try. The more you do these things, the more likely they are to become second nature. Eventually you won't even have to think about doing them; they will come naturally.

# Males Are Victims Too

Rape is not only a female problem. Males are involved in rape in many ways. The most obvious way is as assailants, and in fact most rapes are committed by men. But males as children and adults are also victims of sexual assault. Some men who sexually assault others were themselves victims of sexual assault as children.

In his book *Men Who Rape*[1], Nicholas Groth writes that the two most important aspects of manhood are strength and sexuality, and when a man has been raped he has lost both or may feel that he has. In addition, men may be the fathers, lovers, brothers, or friends of rape victims. Men may be linked in many ways to rape.

Rape is not something men talk about very much, perhaps because they are not comfortable talking about their feelings, and rape is a very emotional topic. Men also rarely admit to themselves or each other that they could be victims of rape.

## What If You Were Raped by a Woman?

That is a phenomenon that we seldom hear about, but any man, like any woman, can be the victim of sexual assault.

---

[1] New York: Plenum Press, 1979.

Size, strength, personality, or sexual orientation do not necessarily determine who will be raped. Women can use coercion, force, or violence to get men to have sex against their will. Men sometimes have involuntary erections. Almost every young man has experienced the problem around the beginning of puberty when his hormones were surging. The male hormone testosterone is associated with aggression and sexual drive. High levels of testosterone contribute to erections. So when teenage males have testosterone surges, they often experience erections that they don't want and can't control.

When older men act aggressively or when their testosterone level is high, they also may have uncontrollable erections. Some men experience erections they can't control when they are angry, afraid, or anxious. If a man is with a woman who wants to have sex and threatens him, he may have an erection.

Self-consciousness is the most common cause of impotence. Because of the hormone adrenaline released in dangerous situations, the fear response often overpowers self-consciousness, allowing the erection mechanism to work. But an erection is not necessary for a man to become a victim of sexual assault. A man can be sodomized (forced to have oral or anal sex) against his will without having an erection.

## Eric

*Eric was not very popular on campus and was embarrassed by his lack of friends. He desperately wanted to make friends but didn't know how to go about it. One day in psychology, his lab partner Maria asked him if he would like to join a study group. He* was happy to do so because he thought it would be a good opportunity to get to know some other people and perhaps develop a friendship with Maria.

Maria invited Eric to her house that evening for a study session. When he arrived, four classmates were busily talking about social things. Eric wanted to join in but couldn't think of anything relevant to add. He was feeling more socially inept than ever. Things got better once they started to discuss psychology because Eric had a better grasp of the material than the others.

Eric continued to feel uncomfortable and socially inept, but at a session a few weeks later Maria asked him to stay afterward to help her with a paper. Eric was nervous because he had never been very good with women, but he stayed anyway. After a while she started nuzzling up to him, which made him very uncomfortable, but he didn't know how to make her stop. He decided the best thing to do was to leave, but Maria began to fondle him and kiss him when he said he had to go.

She asked, "What's the matter, don't you like me?" He said he did but he had homework to do. He was very uncomfortable in this situation because he was a virgin. He didn't know what to do sexually, nor did he want to have sex with someone he didn't care about. Maria started to tease him and said there had been rumors in class that he was gay. If he didn't have sex with her, she would know they were true.

Eric was in a panic. He was afraid that if he left, she would tell everyone he was gay. Then he would be rejected by his peers or perhaps even beaten up. He was also embarrassed to tell Maria that he was a virgin.

*He had sex with her unwillingly and felt devastated afterward. She made fun of his awkwardness and difficulty with his erection. He felt used and dirty, but he did not know whom to talk to, or even what to say.*

*He was sure that if he told any man on campus that Maria had forced him to have sex, the response would be, "You lucky guy, I'd give anything to have sex with her. There must be something wrong with you if you had to be forced!" He didn't even know what to call what had happened. He thought rape was something that happened only to women, with male assailants, and that it usually involved force and violence.*

*Eric didn't tell anyone. He just tried to deal with his emotions himself. But it was a long time before he was able to function well in his schoolwork or his personal life.*

Maria used coercion to get Eric to comply, but women can use other ways to get men to have sex against their will. Women can use weapons or the threat of weapons. A woman who has power over a man can threaten abuse of that power; for example, a professor might threaten a failing grade, or a stepmother might withhold an allowance unless the male has sex.

This kind of sexual assault happens much less frequently than men forcing women, which makes it even harder for a male victim to talk about his problem. He may think he is the only one who has had the experience and that no one else will understand. Trained counselors know about these types of situations and can help. More information about where to go for help is given in chapter 11.

# What If You Were Sexually Assaulted by a Man?

Men are sometimes forced to have sex with other men. Many people mistakenly think this proves that the rapist and the victim are homosexual. In reality, just as in the case of women victims, rape of men is usually motivated by a desire to dominate someone weaker or a compulsion to replay childhood experiences of sexual abuse. Many people think that a man who can be forced to have sex with another man must be unmanly, weak, gay, or all three, and that a "real man" would fight the rapist off. This may not be possible if the rapist overpowers you or has a weapon. It is especially difficult if there is more than one assailant.

Most rapes of men by other men take place in prison. Men who rape men would probably choose women as victims if they were available. Since women are not available, they choose men whom they can dominate, manipulate, and degrade. If you asked rapists of men if they considered themselves homosexual, most would say no.

Some men who have been raped by other men believe that such an act is sexual and must imply something about the sexuality of the victim. The person who was raped may think that something about him attracted the rapist and therefore he must have homosexual tendencies.

In fact, something probably did draw the rapist to the victim, but it had nothing to do with sexual orientation. Rapists seek people they can dominate. If the victim appeared unsure of himself, lonely, or unhappy, the rapist may have assessed him as someone who wouldn't put up much of a fight.

Being raped by someone of your own sex does not mean anything about your sexual orientation. It is important to understand that rape is primarily an act of violence and only incidentally sexual. If someone beats you in the process of stealing your car, you are a victim of a violent crime. In the same way, if you are the victim of sexual assault by a man, it doesn't make you any more or less homosexual or heterosexual. It means you are the victim of a crime, not a willing sex partner. You may, however, feel less like having sex with anyone after the assault, because any nonconsensual activity involving the genitals is associated with the devastating experience of loss of control. Gradually, as you work through that loss and feel more in control again, sex will be more appealing.

## Responses to Sexual Assault

Men who have been sexually assaulted report feeling ashamed of not having avoided the attack or of being involved in a "perverse" sexual act. They often feel dirty and emasculated. They may feel degraded or disgusted, and begin to question their sexual orientation and their masculinity.

Rape victims, whether male or female, need emotional help to deal with what happened to them and to regain healthy behavior patterns. Most Rape Crisis Centers have male and female counselors trained to help you with the emotions you experience after rape or sexual assault. Also, a supportive and understanding friend or family member may be able to help you sort things out. Other

159

professionals in your community can help. Selecting the best support people is described in chapter 11.

Men who have been victims of sexual assault often have trouble with their sexuality, or they may have sex with as many women as possible to prove to themselves that they are "normal." If they fear that they are gay, they may try to avoid any sexual feelings for fear of being aroused by other men. The fact is that one sexual encounter (voluntary or forced) with another man does not make you gay. Sexual orientation is determined in early life, and one act later in life will not change that.

## Reporting

Studies show that men are much more likely to report rape if they tried to fight back, perhaps because they are less likely to be blamed if there is evidence of a fight. Many men won't accept counseling, considering it unmanly and an admission of helplessness. On the contrary, a trained counselor can help you regain your sex drive and feelings of power and self-esteem. If it will help you regain your strength and sex drive, what could be more masculine?

# Why Do Nice Men Force Friends to Have Sex?

There are different types of sexual sharing. Sex when both partners are willing is called consensual sex. Sex when one person agrees to gratify the other person, but will not receive pleasure in the act, is called altruistic sex. In complaint sex, one partner complains that he or she does not want sex but the other continues until satisfied (most acquaintance rape falls into this category). The last category is rape, where sex is clearly forced, or violence or coercion is used. Acquaintance rape may be either complaint sex or rape.

If you know someone who has raped and you don't do anything about it or you condone it, you are condoning rape in general. Taken one step further, sexist jokes (in which women are dehumanized or degraded) and violence towards women are forms of behavior that make rape seem more acceptable to men who may have the tendency to rape. It is hard to condemn sexist or pro-rape attitudes in groups where those attitudes are the norm. Unfortunately, when men get together they often make sexist jokes or discuss women as objects.

Most people do not know the legal definition of rape, nor do they know exactly what constitutes rape. Many men assume that they have never raped because they think rape is a violent act committed by a stranger. In learning the definition and discussing what behaviors constitute rape, many men might have to face the fact that they have forced a woman to do something sexual against her will. In other words, they may have raped.

## What If You Committed Rape?

Many men who commit acquaintance or date rape do not know they have committed a crime. Remember, the definition of rape is forcing a woman to have intercourse without her consent or if she is fearful for her life or afraid of injury. She is not able to consent if she is unconscious, asleep, under seventeen years of age (in most states), or mentally incompetent. If you forced, threatened, used violence, or coerced a woman to have sex under any of those circumstances, it was rape.

Men tend to assign a sexual meaning to certain behaviors that women would consider friendly. For example, if a woman invites a man to her apartment for a beverage after a date, she may merely want to be friendly. Her date may assume that it is meant as a sexual come-on and think he has "a right" to force her to have sex. Therefore, she will have to put up active resistance because he assigned his own meaning to her behavior.

Men often blame women for causing rape. Psychiatric views have even included blaming an overbearing or "cold" mother, "frigid" wives, or "provocative" victims. These ideas ignore the fact that the man has free will. He can choose to rape or not rape.

In other situations, mental illness, alcoholism, or uncontrollable impulse have been cited as reasons for rape. In most cases, especially acquaintance rape, the assailant has no clear signs of mental illness. He is able to control his other impulses in life, and if he does not, he is held accountable for them. For example, if he had an impulse to shoot a neighbor's dog he would be arrested, not excused because he couldn't control himself, because he'd been drinking, or because he was mentally ill.

Alcohol is often involved in acquaintance rape situations, but it does not justify rape. Some people excuse a man for forcing a woman to have sex when he was drunk because "he couldn't help himself," as though he were like a runaway train that can't be stopped. Men are held accountable for committing other crimes while drunk, and the same standards are applicable in rape situations. The law does not consider drunkenness a defense.

Finally, men have been excused from the charge of rape because of "victim precipitation," which means that the victim caused the rape. In no other situation do we dismiss a crime because of the victim's behavior. For example, if a man walks in a bad part of town and is mugged, we do not excuse the crime because he shouldn't have been there. But in acquaintance rape, the assailant is too often excused if the victim went to his apartment willingly.

In a survey of high school students, researchers found that males were more likely than females to think a non-verbal action had a sexual meaning. More than one-third of the males thought it was acceptable to force a woman to have sex if she had "led him on," if he had spent a lot of money on her, if he knew she had had sexual intercourse with other men, if he was "so turned on he couldn't stop," if she was intoxicated, if she let him touch her above the waist, or if they had been dating a long time.

More than half thought that forced sex was acceptable if she changed her mind; that is, first said yes and then decided she didn't want it.

The fact of the matter is that women are never responsible for being victims of rape. The person who forces sex is the one who is responsible for the rape. None of the above "acceptable" conditions are moral, ethical, or legal reasons for forcing someone to have sex.

Some men justify forced sex if a woman was drinking and passed out, saying that she was asking for it. This is not true according to the law. And if one thinks about the situation, it's hard to imagine how one can ask for something when unconscious.

Some men fall back on the fiction that a woman never really means no in a sexual situation. But if a woman did say no and did mean it and was then forced to have sex, she was raped. Still others maintain that if a woman has had consensual sex with a man in the past, he "has a right" to sex with her again. The law makes no reference to previous sexual experiences with the victim; previous acts, consensual or forced, are irrelevant.

Some people believe the myth that rape happens only when a stranger jumps out of the bushes and beats a woman in the process of forcing her to have sex. In fact, rape without obvious violence by an assailant who knows the victim occurs much more often than stranger rape.

## Brian

*Sue was a very sexy young woman whom Brian met at a party. He had been hearing about her for weeks* from his buddies on the hockey team, who said she was "loose" and interested in many sexual practices. Sue was a real hockey fan and went to all the games. After one game when Brian made a winning goal, Sue called to say that she was very impressed and would like to help him celebrate. Was he available to go to a party with her next Friday night? Brian said yes and hurried to tell his buddies about his date. They immediately started telling him about all the sexual activities he had to look forward to with Sue.

When Friday finally came, Brian picked Sue up and they went to the party. She drank a lot and danced very seductively. At the end of the party she invited Brian to her house for something to drink. She said that her roommates were out of town for the weekend.

They were both pretty drunk when they got there, but they continued drinking. Brian started to kiss and undress her, and Sue seemed to be enjoying it. When he tried to take her pants off, she told him no, but he thought she was playing hard to get. Besides, he had heard that she was into S & M (kinky forced sex). He continued to try to undress her, and she fought harder. Brian couldn't understand why she would want to be forced, but he felt sure he was giving her what she wanted.

He finally succeeded in having intercourse with her after a half hour of struggle. She stopped resisting when he was kneeling on her legs and holding her arms down. The next day in the locker room he proudly reported the events of the previous evening to his teammates.

Brian thought the date was great, but Sue was raped. In reality, she usually refused sex, and because of that a few angry and rejected dates had started rumors about her. Brian believed that she had had sex with everyone else and assumed that she would want him too. He believed that the messages she gave proved that she was a loose young woman: She called him up for the date, she drank a lot, she danced suggestively, she invited him to her house, and she told him her roommates were away for the weekend. Brian wanted sex and he wanted to believe that she wanted it too, so he decided that no must be part of a sexual game she was playing. Since he was drunk, he was not able to assess the situation correctly.

Brian may never know that he raped Sue. If he does find out, he may deny it, or he may feel terrible because he believes himself to be a kind and moral person.

## What Are Your Feelings?

After reading this chapter, if you believe you may have forced someone to have sex you may be feeling bad about having committed rape. You may need to talk to a counselor to help you understand what actually happened and how you should change your behavior to avoid raping again. You may want to think about how to interact with your partner in the future. Some communities have men's discussion groups that deal with these issues. You may also find the book *Men on Rape* by Timothy Beneke[1] helpful.

---

[1] New York: St. Martin's Press, 1982.

# How Can You Help to Avoid Rape?

If you think you may have committed acquaintance rape and you want to make sure you don't do it again, there are several things you can do. You can work toward changing your behavior. You can also talk to other men about the issue and help them learn ways to change their behavior, and stress the importance of doing so.

### Use Peer Pressure in a Positive Way

Men often use peer pressure to reinforce negative behaviors regarding women and sex. For example, men ask each other, "How far did you get last night?" That kind of question puts pressure on the man to make sure he has something to report to his buddies, regardless of the woman's wishes. If he didn't have sex with her, he may lie about it, thereby giving her a "bad reputation." When other men go out with her they will expect the same treatment that their friend reported, whether it was true or not. So the woman may be forced to have sex by a second man, because he believes she had sex with the first man and he is angry that she says no to him.

Rather than asking a friend how far he got with a date, you can ask him if he enjoyed her company and if they liked the movie. Think of the young woman as a person rather than a sex object, and encourage your friends to do the same.

If you hear your friends talking about a woman as a sex object, tell them you don't like to hear women put down in that way. Try to help them understand the problem with such behavior. Be sure to suggest alternative ways of discussing these issues.

## Meet Your Need for Intimacy Through Other Men

One reason men feel they need to have sex so often is that our society does not offer them many other options to fulfill their need for intimacy. If men could be more comfortable having emotionally close friends, they would not need to turn to sex to substitute physical closeness for emotional closeness. Unfortunately, this kind of behavior is not encouraged. Men are often afraid to share their feelings for fear of being thought weak or unmanly. Whether they talk about them or not, almost all men have feelings of pain, insecurity, and rejection. Sharing those feelings with other men can help a man discover that he is not alone and that the feelings are normal. Most communities have men's groups that advocate developing close emotional relationships between men.

Some men are afraid to develop such relationships because they associate emotional closeness between men with homosexuality. Although some homosexual men have relationships that are emotionally close, not all do. Conversely, heterosexual men can also have very close emotional relationships with other men. Emotional sharing does not necessitate sexual sharing, nor does a man's sharing of emotions mean that he is a sissy or gay. It does, however, expand his options of human interaction and will probably keep him healthier in the long run because supportive relationships reduce stress.

## Understand That Sex Is Not Emotional Intimacy

Many people assume that sexual intercourse automatically involves emotional intimacy. The two may go hand in hand, but often do not. Think of the people to whom you feel closest: perhaps your mother, brother, a teammate, a teacher, your best friend. What is it about those relationships that causes you to feel close? Sex is probably not the reason. There are other factors that foster emotional intimacy, like sharing feelings, discussing important events and moments, and helping each other during difficult times.

Many people have one-time sexual encounters, commonly referred to as "one-night stands." They know very little about the person they have sex with. Sex itself does not make an encounter emotionally intimate. They may have shared physical intimacy but no emotional intimacy. If what you need is an emotionally intimate relationship, you need to share feelings and experiences, not simply sex. Sexual encounters that have no emotional component will leave you disappointed and feeling empty, especially if you were in need of emotional intimacy.

## Respect Your Partner

Many acquaintance rapes occur because the man thinks he has more of a right to his desires than does his partner. This usually happens if he believes he is "better" than his partner. One way to avoid acquaintance rape is to date only women who you think are equal to you. If you can't find such dates, perhaps you should reconsider what it is that makes someone important and valuable to you. Perhaps your priorities need to be redefined.

## Listen to the Messages Your Partner Gives

People can give messages in two ways, verbal and nonverbal (body language). We often rely on body language to know what a person really means, but unfortunately we do not always interpret the message correctly. In a sexual situation, for example, a woman's no may be interpreted as no, maybe, or yes. How does a man interpret the word if he doesn't believe she means what she says? Is it her inflection, her accompanying hand gestures, her tone of voice, what she does with her body, her past behavior, or a combination of several of these? If you read the cues wrong, you may make the wrong judgment. Most of us are not good mind readers when we want something so much that it clouds our ability to understand that our partner does not want the same thing.

Suppose you base your decision on past behavior and believe that no means yes, but this time she really means no. Perhaps something is different about her situation today; she does not feel well, she is worried about not having a means of birth control, or she just isn't in the mood. Just because no meant yes in the past does not mean it ever will again.

Suppose she giggles when she says no and you take that to mean that she is not serious. Perhaps her giggle means that she is ticklish, or nervous about what you are doing. You can't assume that anything you believe to be inconsistent body and verbal language gives you the green light.

A better way to handle the situation would be to stop what you are doing the first time she says no. If she really meant no she will be delighted that you stopped. If she meant maybe or yes, she will wonder what you are doing. She may say, "Why did you stop?" and you can respond, "Because you said no." If she says she didn't really mean no, she will have to take the responsibility if she wants to continue. An advantage of that is that you will not be in the usual position of facing possible rejection. If she is the one to initiate, she will be the one facing rejection. In addition, you will never have to wonder if you have forced someone to do something she didn't want to do. And you won't face the possibility of having a police officer show up at your home to arrest you for committing a rape that you didn't think you committed.

You can also be honest and ask a woman if she would like to go to bed with you, if that's your intention. Consider something like, "Why don't we go to my apartment where we can be alone and go to bed if we both agree?"

## You Too Can "Have a Headache"

One reason men force women to have sex is that many men feel pressured always to be ready and willing to have sex. A man may think, "No matter what the circumstances, the evening has to end in a sexual encounter or I have failed." He feels forced to be what he thinks is "normal." Being normal means doing what feels right for you.

## Understand the Law

Not knowing that what you did was wrong won't save you from having to deal with the criminal justice system. If you break the law, you are likely to have to pay the consequences. Acquaintance and date rape are against the law. Men who commit acquaintance rape are frequently surprised to be arrested and indicted for a serious crime. The long-term consequences of a felony conviction are serving time in prison, having a criminal record, and losing your reputation. If you are arrested but not indicted, others may still know that you have been suspected of the crime and may view you differently. It could also hurt your chances for a job if the application asks whether you have ever been arrested.

## Conclusion

Acquaintance rape and sexual assault are crimes that affect men as being important people in the lives of the victims, as victims themselves, or as assailants. It is crucial for men to learn as much as possible about rape and sexual assault prevention. Following are important points that all men should know:

1. Rape is a crime of violence motivated by the desire to control and dominate.

2. It is never acceptable to force yourself on a woman, even if you think she has been leading you on or you have heard that women say no but mean yes.

3. When you use force to have sex, you are committing a crime even if you know the woman or have had sex with her before.

4. You don't have to initiate sex; you can say no too.

5. Whenever a partner says no—stop! Otherwise you may be committing rape.

6. The best way to avoid rape is to have a clear, honest discussion with your partner about sexual intimacy and protection against pregnancy and sexually transmitted diseases.

# Let's Put a Stop to It!

Is it possible to stop the growing problems of sexual assault and sexual harassment among teenagers? Reforms are necessary in four different areas to stem the tide of these serious problems: legislation and law, education, socialization, and the mass media. The goal is constructively and positively to create attitudes as well as behavior changes that will reduce the incidence of these problems.

## Sex Role Socialization

Traditional sex roles contribute significantly to a societal environment in which sexual harassment and sexual assault are simply part of the social fabric. Male dominance and female passivity encourage forced sex situations by teaching men that they should take what they want, and teaching women that it is their obligation to provide men with what they want.

Teenagers of today are the parents, lawmakers, teachers, coaches, and jurors of tomorrow. Adults who interact with children and adolescents help form their attitudes and behaviors by what they say and, even more importantly, by what they do. Today's teenagers are tomorrow's role models. Young people today must understand the dysfunctional aspects of traditional sex role stereotypes and work to change them for their own generation as well as for generations to come.

## Educational Area

Education can influence sex role socialization in a variety of ways. Educators must be hypersensitive to gender issues. For example, both boys and girls can excel in math and science, and boys as well as girls may be exceptionally good in early childhood education and nursing. It is important for all children to receive the same opportunities, encouragement, and discouragement in school, regardless of gender. To be most effective in changing attitudes and behaviors, these ideas need to be introduced in preschool, not high school. By the time a person has reached high school, most of his or her social attitudes have already been formed. Schools also need to implement credible, age-appropriate, interesting sexual assault and sexual harassment prevention education. Both males and females must be the targets of these educational efforts, and the programs must be interactive and focus on feelings, not just teach facts through a lecture format.

Both males and females need to learn assertiveness skills. In this culture, girls tend to be socialized to be passive and manipulative (especially in social relationships), whereas boys are socialized to be aggressive and manipulative. Neither gender receives general assertiveness training. Schools are one place where assertiveness may be taught to everyone. Teachers and administrators may not like the outcome of effective assertiveness training, because the students will have more skills to get what they want in interactions with their teachers. Our culture as a whole would benefit enormously if all people had assertiveness skills and could make their wishes clear without anger or violence.

Schools also need to train educational staff to investigate reports of sexual harassment and sexual assault. Schools must first develop specific policies regarding reporting protocol for inappropriate behaviors.

## Legislative and Legal Areas

The legislative branch of the government must reinforce egalitarian gender roles and discourage sexually offensive and exploitative behaviors in policies, regulations, and laws. As long as people are able to get away with sexual harassment and forcing sex, they lack the incentive to stop those behaviors. Laws must be passed that make it illegal to commit those behaviors under all circumstances, not only if the victim and assailant are not married to each other. Laws should also require schools to provide education regarding these issues. The penalties should be stiff for offenders, and effective sex offender treatment programs should be available to keep the offenders from repeating their crimes once they leave prison. Funds must be allocated legislatively for all of above efforts.

However, unless judges, district attorneys, and juries believe that these crimes are unacceptable, the legislative changes will not have the impact of reducing these behaviors. Therefore, the media, educational, and sex role socialization changes must all happen simultaneously for the legal system to contribute positively to the reduction of unwanted sexual behaviors.

Judges have been known to lecture victims that they should not have dressed so provocatively if they didn't want to have sex. Juries have acquitted a defendant despite overwhelming evidence that he committed a sexual offense, because he was from a nice family and the victim was from "the wrong side of the tracks." District attorneys have refused to take cases because they didn't think their chances of winning were good; perhaps because they were more interested in their conviction rate than in seeing justice done. Many rape victims choose not to go to the police about a rape because they are afraid of the treatment they are likely to receive from the criminal justice system. Not only are these situations sometimes realities, they are also portrayed as commonplace by the media.

## Media Influence and Responsibility

The mass media currently contribute to a "rape culture" by depicting sexual harassment and sexual assault as commonplace. In a 1992 study of sexual violence in Hollywood movies, one out of eight of films depicts a rape, and by the time a person reaches the age of eighteen in the United States, he or she will have seen an average of 250,000 acts of violence on television (Linz et al., 1992). By the time young people reach college, they report that media figures and peers (in that order) are their most common role models for sexual behavior (Fabes and Strouse, 1987).

Research has demonstrated that excessive exposure to rape and murder does influence adolescents' sexual attitudes and behaviors. Unfortunately, media role models tend to represent irresponsible models of sexual behavior; they often emphasize lack of communication between partners, male dominance and female subservience, sexual violence, and rape-prone attitudes (such as "If she didn't want to have sex with him, she wouldn't have gone to his room").

The mass media can take it upon themselves to present more responsible depictions of interpersonal relationships, but this is probably unlikely in the near future. We can boycott the films that depict sexual violence, sexual harassment, and dysfunctional interpersonal interactions, as well as boycotting the products that are advertised in or during sexually violent presentations.

There are two educational approaches to reducing the impact that sexually violent movies and television shows have on the viewers. The first is to debrief the audience after the film. This is extremely labor-intensive and requires a receptive audience to stay for the debriefing. The second is pre-film viewing, which requires an informed instructor to comment on the sexually violent portions of the film before it is shown in entirety. It is necessary to intersperse the actual clips of film with clips from real life during the pre-film viewing in order to influence the viewers (Linz et al., 1992). These methods will have most impact if they are used in conjunction with educational programs in schools that teach adolescents about sexual violence and sex role stereotypes.

## Conclusion

Adolescents from all regions throughout the world may be involved in sexual harassment and sexual assault, either as victims or assailants. The current structure of our society encourages traditional sex roles, where males are dominant and females are submissive. In order to break this mold, education and the media must infiltrate the socialization process and empower both males and females to communicate with one another more directly. The media must take responsibility for the excessive sexual violence that they bring into our lives and take action to curb the negative effects. Females must be taught how to be assertive with dating partners, rather than not knowing how to make their wishes understood. Males must learn to be assertive rather than aggressive in sexual encounters and be willing to take no for an answer. Legislative and legal changes are necessary to reinforce responsible sexual behaviors. Sexual harassment and sexual assault between acquaintances will not end unless males and females teach each other how to listen, communicate, and understand one another.

# Glossary

**acquaintance rape** Forced sexual intercourse (or other sexual act) between two people who know each other.

**aggravated rape** Rape in which a weapon, threat, violence, or force is used.

**aggression** Demanding one's wishes without regard for the rights of others.

**anger rapist** Rapist who is angry at women in general or one woman in particular.

**assertiveness** Asking for your wishes without violating the rights of others.

**civil suit** Legal action in which a victim sues the assailant personally.

**consensual sex** Sexual intercourse (or other sexual act) between two willing partners.

**criminal prosecution** Legal action in which the state prosecutes a defendant.

**crisis phase** Stage of the rape trauma syndrome that follows immediately after the rape.

**date rape** Forced sexual intercourse (or other sexual act) that occurs between a dating couple or while on a date.

**disorientation phase** Stage of the rape trauma syndrome in which the victim loses emotional balance and has trouble interacting with other people.

**force** Physical violence or threat of violence; coercion or threat of coercion.

**heterosexual** Having sexual interest in persons of the opposite sex.

**homosexual** Having sexual interest in persons of the same sex.

**marital rape** Forced sexual intercourse (or other sexual act) between husband and wife.

**message, nonverbal** Body language that conveys a meaning different from the verbal message given.

**myths, rape** Common but erroneous beliefs about the crime of rape.

**personification** Referring to parts of the body by proper names.

**power rapist** Rapist whose drive is a need to exercise power over a helpless victim.

**rape** Forced sexual intercourse (or other sexual act) against the will of the victim.

**rape shield laws** Statutes that bar revelation in court of a rape victim's previous sexual experience.

**rape trauma syndrome** Series of phases experienced by a victim of rape.

**reorientation phase** Stage in the rape trauma syndrome when the victim begins to regain control of her emotions and life.

**Rohypnol** A drug that causes memory loss and that some rapists use on their victims.

**sadistic rapist** Rapist whose drive is to torture and mutilate his victim.

**sexual assault** Rape, particularly of a male victim.

**sexual intercourse** Penetration of the penis into the vagina.

**simple rape** Rape in which no violence, threat, or struggle occurs.

**socialization** Method by which children are taught their stereotypic sex roles.

**soft rape** Forced sexual intercourse (or other sexual act) in which coercion or threat of coercion is used to gain the victim's compliance.

**stranger rape** Premeditated rape by a person unknown to the victim.

**virgin** A person who has not had consensual sexual relations.

# Where to Go for Help

If you or someone you know has been the victim of rape, help is available. Below are some steps you can take when a rape has occurred.

1. Look up "Rape" in the phone book. You may also find helpful numbers under the listing "Sexual Assault."

2. Call the operator and say that you have been raped and you want to be connected with the Rape Crisis number.

3. Call the YWCA and ask for the nearest Rape Crisis Center.

4. Call a suicide prevention hotline in your area.

5. Contact your school's counseling center or health center.

6. Call the police and ask for the number of a rape counseling center or a specially trained officer who deals with rape.

Contact the following organizations for more information on rape:

**The Rape, Abuse, and Incest National Network (RAINN)**
252 10th Street NE
Washington, DC 20002
(800) 656-HOPE
Web site: http://www.rainn.org

**Smart Date**
P.O. Box 13232
San Luis Obispo, CA 93401
Web site: http://www.smartdate.com

# For Further Reading

AAUW. *Hostile Hallways: The AAUW Survey on Sexual Harassment in America's Schools.* Washington, DC: American Association of University Women, 1993.

Bart, P. *Stopping Rape: Successful Survival Strategies.* New York: Pergamon Press, 1985.

Benedict, H. *Recovery: How to Survive Sexual Assault for Women, Men, Teenagers, Their Friends and Families.* Garden City, NY: Doubleday & Company, 1985.

Beneke, Timothy. *Men on Rape: What They Have to Say About Sexual Violence.* New York: St. Martin's Press, 1982.

Brownmiller, S. *Against Our Will: Men, Women and Rape.* New York: Simon & Schuster, 1975.

Burt, M. R. "Rape Myths and Acquaintance Rape." In A. Parrot and L. Bechhofer, eds., *Acquaintance Rape: The Hidden Crime.* New York: John Wiley & Sons, 1991.

Eskenazi, G. "Male Athletes and Sexual Assault." *Cosmopolitan,* February 1991.

Estrich, Susan. *Real Rape: How the Legal System Victimizes Women Who Say No.* Cambridge, MA: Harvard University Press, 1987.

Fabes, R. A., and Strouse, J. "Perceptions of responsible and irresponsible models of sexuality: A correctional study." *Journal of Sex Research,* 23(1), 70-84, 1987.

Finkelhor, D. *Child Sexual Abuse: New Theory and Research.* New York: The Free Press, 1984.

Groth, Nicholas A. *Men Who Rape: The Psychology of the Offenders.* New York: Plenum Press, 1979.

Koss, M. P., C. A. Gidycz, and N. Wisniewski. "The Scope of
    Rape; Incidence and Prevalence of Sexual Aggression and
    Victimization in a National Sample of Higher Education
    Students." *Journal of Consulting and Clinical Psychology,*
    55(2), 162-170.

Koss, M., and M. Harvey. *The Rape Victim: Clinical and
    Community Approaches to Treatment.* Lexington, MA:
    Stephen Greene Press, 1987.

Linz, D., B. Wilson, and E. Donnerstein. "Sexual violence in
    the mass media: Legal solutions, warnings and mitigation
    through education." *Journal of Social Issues,* 48(1), 145-
    171, 1992.

Malamuth, N. "Rape Proclivity Among Males." *Journal of
    Social Issues,* 37 (1981), 138-157.

Miller, B., and J. C. Marshall. "Coercive Sex on the University
    Campus." *Journal of College Student Personnel,* 28
    (1987), 38-46.

Muehlenhard, C. L., and S. C. Cook. "Men's Self Reports of
    Unwanted Sexual Activity." *The Journal of Sex Research,*
    24 (1988), 58-72.

Muehlenhard, C., and R. McFall. "Dating Initiation from a
    Woman's Perspective." *Behavior Therapy,* 12, 1981.

Neimark, J. "Out of Bounds? The Truth About Athletes and
    Rape." *Mademoiselle,* May 1991.

Parrot, A. "Do Rape Education and Prevention Programs
    Influence Patterns Among New York State College
    Students?" Paper presented at the 1990 Annual Meeting
    of the Society for the Scientific Study of Sex, Minneapolis,
    MN, November 1990.

———. "A Comparison of Male and Female Sexual Assault
    Victimization Experiences Involving Alcohol." Paper pre-
    sented at the 1992 Annual Convention of the Society of
    the Scientific Study of Sex, San Diego, CA.

Parrot, A., and L. Bechhofer, eds. *Acquaintance Rape: The*

*Hidden Crime.* New York: John Wiley and Sons, 1991.

Parrot, A., N. Cummings, and T. Marchell. *Rape 101: Sexual Assault Prevention for College Athletes.* Holmes Beach, FL: Learning Publications, Inc., 1994.

Pritchard, C. *Avoiding Rape On and Off Campus,* 2nd ed. Wenonah, NJ: State College Publishing Company, 1987.

Rowland, Judith. *The Ultimate Violation—Rape Trauma Syndrome: An Answer for Victims, Justice in the Courtroom.* New York: Doubleday and Company, 1985.

Rubenstein, C. "Fighting sexual harassment in schools." *New York Times,* June 3, 1993.

Smith, Susan E. *Fear or Freedom: A Woman's Options in Social Survival and Physical Defense.* Racine, WI: Mother Courage Press, 1986.

Strauss, S., and P. Espeland. *Sexual Harassment and Teens.* Minneapolis: Free Spirit Publishing, Inc., 1992.

Strouse, T., and Fabes, R.A. "Formal vs. informal sources of sexuality education: Competing forces in the sexual socialization process." *Adolescence,* 20, 251-263, 1985.

Struckman-Johnson, C. "Male Victims of Acquaintance Rape." In A. Parrot and L. Bechhofer, eds., *Acquaintance Rape: The Hidden Crime.* New York: John Wiley and Sons, 1991.

# Index

**J**

Johnson, Magic, 70
jokes, sexist, 13, 17, 161
judgment, questioning one's, 94

**K**

Koss, M. P., 66, 75, 118

**L**

law
  understanding, 171–172
  work to change, 149, 175
legal action, taking, 128–132

**M**

males
  assaulted by males, 158–160
  as victims, 1–2, 20, 26, 28,
    42–43, 100–101,
    125–126, 149, 154–160
  women as rapists of, 154–158
marital rape, 30, 125, 148–149
McFall, Richard, 62
media, influence of, 53–54, 58,
    176–177
memory
  loss of, 5, 8–9
  repression of, 88
*Men on Rape*, 166
*Men Who Rape*, 32–33, 154
messages
  clear, 138–139
  conflicting, 44, 57–58,
    137–138
  "I," 135
  verbal, 55–59, 104, 169–170

Muehlenhard, Charlene, 62, 76
myths
  male sexuality, 63–64
  rape, 25–28, 100, 101, 129,
    150

**N**

National Organization for
    Women, (NOW) 125
no, meaning of, 54–57, 65, 104,
    106–107, 137–138, 164,
    165, 169–71

**O**

objectification, sexual, 17, 19

**P**

partying, 3, 22, 35
peer pressure, 17, 35, 65, 74–75,
    140
  using positively, 167
penis, personifying, 59–60
police
  as counselors, 121–122
  reactions of, 99–101
  reporting to, 25–26, 36, 43,
    66, 160
pornography, violent, 19
power rapist, 32–34
pregnancy, unwanted, 61, 109
  prevention of, 122–123
problems
  emotional, 16, 111
  physical, 16, 122
professional athletes, 72
promiscuity, sexual, 70–71, 104,
    141